THE

TRUTH

AND
THE

REMOVAL

THE SECOND COMING OF JESUS CHRIST
and
THE ASSASSINATION OF PRESIDENT JAMES A. GARFIELD

By
CHARLES J. GUITEAU

MCLOUD, OK:
COBB PUBLISHING
2016

Kindle Edition available at Amazon.com.

Guiteau, Charles Julius (1841-1882), American Assassin of President James A. Garfield.

ISBN-13: 978-0692673072
ISBN-10: 0692673075

PUBLISHER'S PREFACE

Charles Guiteau, best-known for being the assassin whose bullet led to the death of President James A. Garfield in 1881, had, prior to that occasion, written a book on the second coming of Jesus Christ, called "The Truth." It is said that he plagiarized most of the material from Noyes, but that it also expressed Guiteau's theological beliefs isn't denied. A look at the titles of Part One of this book will give you some insight into his thoughts on the issue.

After his conviction of murdering the President, he tried to drum up financial support for an appeal by re-releasing *The Truth*, and accompanying it with a second section on "The Removal" of Garfield. For the person interested in American history, this section is fascinating, especially the newspaper reports that state that the assassination of the President actually saved the United States from engaging in a planned war with Chile.

In preparing this work, we have modernized the spelling, corrected typographical errors, updated the formatting for Bible references ("ii, 24" is now "2:24"), and given the whole book a visual facelift.

This book is much different from what we normally publish, but we have decided to bring it to press because we believe the discerning reader can benefit from it. Even though we do not agree with all that Guiteau said in the first part, there are some very good thoughts interspersed (such as the comparison of Paul and Nero on pages 18-19). Additionally, his eschatological beliefs (a modified form of *Preterism*) are being promoted again by others; and thus it is useful for understanding *why* some of these doctrines are held.

The second part contains a very potent example of what happens when man claims to know the will of God apart from His inspired Scriptures. Charles Guiteau's legal defense was that the Diety (God) forced him to shoot Garfield, and that he was therefore not acting of his own accord. How many times have we heard or read about people who claim "God told me to…" in an effort to justify their sinful actions?

Ultimately, we are publishing this book because we like American history and religious history—and this one has both, as Guiteau (and others) believed that assassinating the only U.S. President who had also been a preacher was something God wanted done.

Obviously, we do not endorse the actions of Guiteau in murdering Garfield, nor do we endorse his off-the-wall theological beliefs. But we certainly do find this book interesting. We hope you find it interesting as well.

Bradley S. Cobb, Editor.
March, 2016

CONTENTS

PART ONE: THE TRUTH
ABOUT THE SECOND COMING OF JESUS CHRIST

PART TWO: THE REMOVAL OF
PRESIDENT JAMES A. GARFIELD

APPENDIX

PART I
THE

TRUTH

A COMPANION TO THE BIBLE

PREFACE.

I was on theology two or three years, and this book is the result. It was written as I had light during this period. "Christ's Second Coming, A.D. 70," was written at the Public Library in Chicago in December, 1876. I worked a month on it. "'Paul the Apostle" and "Christianity Reviewed" were written in Milwaukee, Wisconsin, in August and September, 1878. "A Reply to Attacks on the Bible" and "Hades and the Final Judgment" were mostly written at Bridgeport, Ct. in February, 1878. "Some Reasons Why Many People are Going Down to Perdition" was written at the Library of the Young Men's Christian Association in the city of New York in September, 1879. "The Two Seeds" was written at "The Arlington," in Washington, D.C. in June, 1881.

"The Truth" is my contribution to the civilization of the race, and I ask for it a careful attention, to the end, that many souls may find the Savior. A new line of thought runs through it, and if it does not demonstrate the existence of Heaven and Hell, I submit their existence cannot be proved.

CHARLES GUITEAU.
United States Jail,
Washington, D.C. *March* 6, 1882.

PAUL THE APOSTLE

THE life of a great man, in a great period of the world's history, is a subject to command the attention of every thoughtful mind. Alexander, on his Eastern expedition, spreading the civilization of Greece over the Asiatic and African shores of the Mediterranean; Julius Caesar, contending against the Gauls, and subduing the barbarism of Western Europe to the order and discipline of Roman government; Charlemagne, compressing the separating atoms of the feudal world, and reviving for a time the image of imperial unity; Columbus, sailing westward over the Atlantic to discover a new world which might receive the arts and religion of the old; Napoleon, on his rapid campaigns, shattering the ancient systems of European States and leaving a chasm between our present and the past—these *(says an historian)* are the colossal figures of history, which stamp their personal greatness on the centuries in which they lived.

But I tell you of a greater than they. I tell you of Jesus Christ, and of Paul His great apostle. Compared to Christ and Paul, the greatest men of the world sink into insignificance. They lived and thrived for a time in power, in wealth, in luxury, and then they went down. When all things were ripe, Paul came. He came at the confluence of three national civilizations—the Roman, the Greek, and the Jewish. The Romans represented temporal power and pleasure. The Greeks sought wisdom; the Jews religion. Aside from the Jews, the whole world was given to idolatry. For two thousand years God had sent upon the Jewish nation the rain and sunshine of religious discipline. They were his chosen people. The Old Testament is the record of God's dealings with the Jews during these two thousand years.

When the time came, in the providence of God, for the long-promised and much-looked-for Messiah to appear in the flesh, Jesus of Nazareth was born of the Virgin Mary. In time this God-man grew to manhood. Then came John the Baptist, preaching in the wilderness of Judea, "Repent, for the kingdom of God is at hand." Then Christ himself began to preach, "Repent, for the kingdom of God is at hand." He moved up and down Judea, "and spake as one having authority." Vast multitudes followed him. He cast out devils, healed the sick, restored the blind and diseased, told the multitude who He was, and what He came for; that God, the Father, had sent him to point out to the race the way to eternal life.

This wonderful being had nowhere to lay His head. He had no money. He had no friends. He never travelled. He never wrote a book. He was hated, despised, and finally crucified as a vile impostor. Then, back He went to the bosom of His Father. The natural eye of man has never seen Him since (except for a brief time when He appeared to His disciples after His resurrection). He gathered to himself a few despised individuals who believed that He was "God manifested in the flesh." They were as poor as Himself. They had no money and no standing in society, and were mostly fishermen. He told them that after He was gone, something (He called it the Holy Spirit) would come upon them and fill them with power. By it they could cast out devils and do mightier works than He had done.

His disciples went about telling that the Jews had made a terrible mistake in crucifying this wonderful being. That he was in truth the Son of the living God. Many believed it, and trembled with great fear when they realized they had crucified the Lord of glory. There was some doubt about His resurrection. He said He should rise again "in three days." Some believed it; some did not; and there were great disputings about it. Some even in this age deny His resurrection. But most decent people believe it. "If Christ be not risen," says Paul, "then is our preaching vain." "Ye are yet in your sins." It is of the utmost importance to know if this wonderful being was raised from the dead, as He said He would be and as most people believe He was. The salvation or damnation of individuals rests upon their belief of this point.

This wonderful being spake as man never spake before (nor since). His ideas appalled his hearers. He claimed greater wisdom than Moses. The Jews could not stand His teachings. They never had heard anything like it, and it made them *mad.* "Art thou greater than our Father Abraham?" "What makest thou thyself?" "Tell us, 'Who art thou?'"

The teachings of this wonderful being were taken up by one Saul, a man of great intellect and learning. He was miraculously converted on his way to Damascus, whither he was going, "breathing out threatenings and slaughter against the disciples of the Lord." As he journeyed near Damascus, suddenly there shone about him a light from heaven, and he fell to the earth, as in a trance, and he heard a voice saying, "Saul, Saul, why persecutest thou me?" And he said, "Who art thou, Lord? And the Lord said, I am Jesus, whom thou persecutest. *It is* hard for thee to kick against the pricks." (Acts, 9:2-5).

"What wilt thou have me to do?" said Paul. The Lord told him his mission, and from that moment, Saul (or Paul as we now call him) was this wonderful being's most devoted follower.

For thirty years, in perils, on the land and on the sea, in daily exposure to death, Paul's devotion to this wonderful being knew neither interruption nor decay. For thirty years, in prison and out of prison, he served him with amazing effect. At all times, and under all circumstances he was true to his Master. His devotion carried him upward and onward, toward an "eternal weight of glory."

I am here to show something of Paul's life and principles.

When God wants anything done, He sends a man to do it. He called Abraham and Moses, and all the leaders of the Old Testament dispensation. When the time came He sent His Son, "Christ Jesus," into this world of sin and misery. For two thousand years He had been preparing the world for His coming. For generations the Old Testament saints had been praying and watching for the Messiah. At last He came, in abject poverty, and "His own received Him not." They entirely mistook the Messiah's mission. They supposed He would relieve them from the Roman yoke, and give them temporal power and pleasure. But Christ came in poverty, to turn the *hearts* of His followers from earth to heaven.

Paul perceived the spiritual nature of Christ's mission, death, and resurrection more than any of His followers. He was learned in the law. His intellect was keen and his spiritual perception, under Divine guidance, most wonderful. His new ideas maddened the Jews. They hated to have their theology upset. It bore the consecrated dust of twenty centuries. It came from their fathers, and they hated to have it set aside. Paul's ideas

14

cut them to the quick, and they sought his life. Religious people hate innovators. They prefer the good old ways of their ancestors.

In the book of Acts we have vivid accounts of the doings of Paul and the apostles while they were trying to introduce Christianity. The Jews fought the innovators at every step. Frequently the apostles were before the ecclesiastical and civil authorities. Sometimes they were scourged, sometimes imprisoned; but out of it all "the Lord delivered them." They kept on preaching. They taught that Jesus of Nazareth, whom the Jews had wickedly crucified, was the true Messiah. Some believed, and some did not. Often a division arose among the Jews as to the guilt or innocence of the apostles, and they escaped punishment on that account. Paul was a Roman citizen, and this fact saved him many scourgings.

Paul was their great preacher. He travelled "from house to house," from city to city, from province to province, warning every man, day and night, "with tears," to find the Savior. He taught publicly and privately. He worked at his trade during the day and preached the Gospel Sundays and at night. He was "all things to all men," working, laboring with his "own hands," that he might not owe any one. At other times "he hungered and thirsted, and was naked, and had no certain dwelling-place." His name became the "offscourings" of the whole world. Whatever his outward circumstances, he stood firm. He called all his troubles "light afflictions." His eye was on the "eternal weight of glory." Under his preaching the Gospel took root. Believers appeared on all sides. Churches were founded in the cities and villages, and Christianity commenced its march toward the conquest of the world.

I desire to put myself in Paul's place, and take you with me through his varied life scenes. Let us go back eighteen centuries. Let us suppose we live in Judea. We find that the Roman government is the only temporal power. All things visible are under its control. Its emperors live in the magnificent city of Rome, in gorgeous palaces, surrounded by retinues of officials, who are their abject slaves. The emperor has absolute control over the life and property of his subjects. His dominions cover

15

nearly the entire earth. His subjects are Romans, Greeks, and Jews. Outside of the Jews, the entire world is given to idolatry and sensuality. Paul was Christ's apostle to the "Gentiles," *i.e.,* to the Romans and Greeks. Peter and the other apostles looked after the Jews. Paul's special work was with the Romans and Greeks. He was to carry the message of eternal life to them. The Romans sought temporal power and pleasure. The Greeks wisdom. Paul, as the preacher of Christianity, had to meet the position of both.

During the reign of Nero, Paul spent two years a prisoner in Rome, and of this experience I shall speak shortly. I now tell how he came to go to Rome.

In the Acts of the Apostles we have a touching account of Paul's charge to the elders of Ephesus, as he goes bound in the spirit unto Jerusalem, not knowing the things that should there befall him, "save that the Holy Ghost witnesseth, that in every city, bonds and afflictions" awaited him. But none of these things moved him. He counted not his life dear unto him. His only anxiety was to finish his Master's work. He told them they should "see his face no more," and that he had faithfully declared unto them "the full counsel of God." "And they all wept sore, and fell on Paul's face, and kissed him, sorrowing most of all that they should see his face no more." (Acts 20:38).

Although repeatedly warned not to go to Jerusalem, Paul went, and, while preaching in the temple, he was apprehended and came very near being mobbed by some Jews from Asia. They moved "all Jerusalem" against him, and only the police saved him from death. They bound him and prepared to scourge him, but desisted, upon finding he was a Roman citizen. He was brought before Felix and charged with being "a pestilent fellow, and a mover of sedition among all the Jews throughout the world, and a ringleader of the sect of the Nazarenes." (Acts 24:5). He denied the accusation, but admitted he "worshipped the God of his fathers" in a way the Jews called heresy. Felix remanded him, hoping to get money. Finally, he appeared before Festus, the successor of Felix, and by him was sent to King Agrippa. Festus sent a letter to the king to the effect that Paul had declared that "one Jesus" was *alive,* whereas in fact he was dead. Then the king wished to see Paul himself, and he was brought before him. Upon a hearing Paul defended himself, and the king was disposed to let him go, but Paul, when before Festus, had appealed to the emperor at Rome, and to him he was sent.

He sailed for Rome under an escort of soldiery, was shipwrecked, but "the Lord stood by him," and all on board were saved. After a time he reached Rome. In Rome he was guarded by a soldier, and lived "two years in his own hired house," preaching the Gospel with "all confidence, no man forbidding him."

Some of Paul's best epistles were written while a prisoner at Rome. Wherever he happened to be, in prison or out of prison, when the spirit moved him he sent an epistle. He always commenced it by declaring his authority as an "Apostle of Jesus Christ, by the will of God, separated unto the Gospel." Sometimes he wrote it with his "own hand." Oftener he dictated it, and sent it by some "dearly beloved" worker "in the Lord." They were publicly read in the churches, often amid "many tears." They were addressed to believers "throughout all ages," and in all conditions of life. His great theme, "Christ crucified—the hope of glory. Dead to the world, alive to God in Christ Jesus." Paul preached the Gospel "in bonds," but the "Word of God" was not bound. It penetrated the confines of the Roman Empire. "Your faith," he says to the Romans, "is spoken of throughout the whole world." (Rom. 1:18).

In the time of Nero—*i.e.,* when Paul was a prisoner in Rome—the Palatine Hill *(says an historian)* had become one vast congeries of imperial piles for the private residence of the emperors and the officials of the court, and for public purposes. It included palaces, temples, libraries, baths, and fountains, the gardens of Adonis, and an area for athletic games. All this pile of palaces was rich beyond all modern luxury, in marble, and gilding, and frescoes, and bronzes, and mosaics, and statuary, and paintings. There, the luxury of life, the extravagance of expenditure in furniture and feasts and wines; the employment of troops of players, mimics, musicians, athletes, gladiators, charioteers, and nameless ministers of nameless vices, were such as Christian civilization, in its most splendid and vicious periods, has never known.

Luxury, lust, and murder went mad in the house of Csesar, from the reign of Augustus to that of Vespasian— *i.e.,* during the very period that Christ and His apostles were trying to establish Christianity.

These emperors were monsters of iniquity. They committed the foulest social vices. They were often vindictive murderers, killing their own relations, without mercy or cause. Nearly all met a violent death. They were too wicked to die like decent men.

But even in "Caesar's household" (*i.e.,* among his slaves), some were called "to the faith of Christ." They loved to hear Paul tell of Jesus and the resurrection. They were servants and slaves, but they were precious to Paul. He knew they would go up and their masters down. "All the saints." he says to Philemon, "salute you. Chiefly they of Caesar's household."

"Not many mighty men" were called in Paul's church. The Gospel was for the poor and needy. The self-righteous Pharisees hated it. The rich and noble missed it, and so it has been in all ages. "I came," says the Master, "not to call the righteous, but sinners to repentance."

Timothy, Paul's beloved son in the Gospel, to whom he wrote two of his most touching and important epistles; also Luke, the writer of the Acts of the Apostles, and Mark, the Evangelist, were among Paul's constant friends while he was a prisoner, "in his own hired house" in Rome. These, and others like minded, surrounded and cheered him by their Christian fellowship and affection. Great indeed must have been the strength which Paul derived from these brethren. Sympathy is sweet in proportion to the bitterness of trials; and their sympathy must have been doubly sweet to Paul, bound as he was "in chains," and living amid a most "awfully polluted Paganism." He speaks of them as "beloved," as "dear," as "faithful," and that "long after" their converts in Christ.

Behold a picture. Look at Paul and the saints in Rome worshiping the God of their fathers, and the new God, Christ Jesus, just revealed to them.

Then look at Nero and his gorgeous surroundings. Nero represented Paganism in its "utmost power, splendor, and corruption." Paul represented Christianity in "its feebleness, poverty, and purity." Nero and Paul represent, each in the highest degree, what the world and the Gospel can do for man. "The one tormented by conscience in the midst of boundless luxury and power; the other, joyful on the verge of martyrdom." The one possessing all temporal good; the other, scarcely nothing. The one rich on earth, but poor in heaven. The other poor here, but rich, for ever and ever, in the eternal world. Think of the infamy on Nero's name all these ages, and then think of the power of Paul's words in the Bible all these centuries. Consider, that they have been read and wept over by millions and millions of the best men and women who have lived "in this vale of tears." Had you rather be Paul or Nero?

"Wives submit yourselves unto your husbands as unto the Lord; husbands, love your wives, as Christ loved the Church," Paul wrote while a Roman prisoner, surrounded by a horrible debauchery and licentiousness.

The Romans had not always been so depraved as they were during the time of Paul and Nero. During the republic, and even in the age of Augustus, the utmost purity prevailed in the family relations. The maidens and matrons were pure and modest. Adultery was punished by death or exile. Even the emperor's own kin were not exempt. Unfortunately this law did not apply to the Roman father or youth. It was only the sanctity of the maidens and matrons that was so sternly guarded; and this, not on the ground of morality, but that the "Roman stock might be preserved unmixed and unweakened," to the end, that the "state might always have fit citizens to uphold and extend the glory of all-conquering Rome." Outside of Roman families great license prevailed. Philosophers counted licentiousness, within the limits of the law, to be unwise, rather than wicked. This was Roman civilization—a civilization which entirely excluded all Divine guidance in the affairs of men.

Paul taught that to break the marriage bond was the greatest of crimes. It was to violate a specific law of God. It was to fill society with pollution, violence, and manifold evil. If his views prevailed, it would close every brothel in the land.

I desire to speak briefly of Paul's second imprisonment in Rome, and his martyrdom.

After being detained two years in Rome, Paul was released. It is supposed he was found "not guilty" of the charges preferred against him by the Jews, and upon which he was held. He preached the Gospel, after his release, in the provinces for several years, but was finally apprehended and sent to Rome the second time, where he was executed under Nero.

It was a terrible time for Paul and his followers, when Nero, mad with debauchery and cruelty, commenced a systematic persecution of the Christians. Rome had been burned, and the opinion prevailed that it had been set on fire by Nero's own orders. The infamy of that horrible transaction still adhered to him. In order, if possible, to remove this imputation, he determined to transfer the guilt to the Christians. They were condemned without sufficient evidence, and put to death with "exquisite cruelty, and to their sufferings Nero offered mockery and derision." The details of this persecution are too horrible for recital, and I pass them by.

I desire to call attention to Paul's spiritual condition while waiting execution. It was during this incarceration that he wrote his second epistle to Timothy, which is so full of faith and apt in expression. It proves the sublime power of the Gospel. It is no less remarkable for what it contains than for what it omits. He tells Timothy, and the faithful "in Christ Jesus," throughout all time, and in all lands, to stand steadfast in the Gospel, and to meet him in heaven. "I charge thee, therefore," he says to Timothy, "before God, and the Lord Jesus Christ, who shall judge the quick and dead at His appearing, to preach the word, in season and out of season, reprove, rebuke, exhort, with long-suffering and doctrine; for the time will come when they will not endure sound doctrine, but turn unto fables. But watch thou in all things, endure afflictions, do the work of an evangelist, make full proof of thy ministry.

"For I am now ready to be offered, and the time of my departure is at hand.

"I have fought a good fight.

"I have finished my course.

"I have kept the faith.

"Henceforth there is laid up for me a crown of righteousness, which the Lord, the righteous judge, shall give me at *that* day; and not to me only, but unto all them, also, that love His appearing." (II Tim. 4:8).

Methinks I see the old warrior in his dungeon in Rome, waiting and watching for his Master. Look at him! Bowed with age. Chained like a condemned felon. Forsaken by "all men." Under sentence of death, and yet he faltered not; for he knew his Master would shortly appear and take him to glory. For thirty years he had proved himself a minister of God, "in much patience, in afflictions, in necessities, in distresses, in stripes, in imprisonments, in tumults, in labors, in watchings, in fastings; by pureness, by knowledge, by long-suffering, by kindness, by the Holy Ghost, by love unfeigned, by the word of truth, by the power of God, by the armor of righteousness, on the right hand and on the left; by honor and dishonor; by evil report and good report; as deceivers, and *yet* true; as unknown, and yet well known; as dying, and behold, we live; as chastened, and not killed; as sorrowful, yet always rejoicing; as poor, yet making many rich; as having nothing, yet possessing all things." (II Cor. 6:4-10).

Yes, yes; thou, Paul, waited only two years for thy "crown." Thou wert executed A.D. 68, and thy Master came at the destruction of Jerusalem, A.D. 70, and gavest thee thy "crown."

CHRIST'S SECOND COMING AT THE DESTRUCTION OF JERUSALEM, A.D. 70.

This was written in December, 1876.

For eighteen centuries Christendom has expected the second coming of Christ. From father to son, from generation to generation, this idea has come down from the primitive Church. During all these ages Christ has *not* appeared in response to this expectation, and we propose to show that the reason He has not appeared is because He came at the siege of Jerusalem, A.D. 70, "in the clouds of heaven, with power and great glory," and judged "the quick and dead," the righteous and wicked of the entire human race (except those living on earth at the *moment* he appeared during the siege of Jerusalem). Those *then* living and *not* taken, and all who have lived on earth since A.D. 70, will be judged at the Final Judgment which will take place at the end of the world.

This is the idea we propose to establish by a careful review of the New Testament, and of Christianity since A.D. 70.

We present the idea that Christ came in judgment at the destruction of Jerusalem, as a discovery, and ask for it a prayerful reception. No one can understand the Bible without *this* view of the Second Coming, and herein is the great value of the discovery.

In examining this subject we wipe away the tradition, and mist, and unbelief of past ages, and stand on the words of Jesus Christ concerning His own coming, and the expectations of Paul, and the primitive Christians. We imagine ourselves with Christ and Paul in Judea. They were addressing common people, and we take them at their words. We believe they said what they meant, and meant what they said.

We have the first reference to Christ's coming in Matthew 10:23. Therein He tells His disciples, "When they persecute you in this city, flee ye into another, for verily, I say unto you, ye shall not have gone over the cities of Israel till the Son of Man come;" in Matthew 16:28, "There be some standing here which shall not taste of death *till* they see the Son of Man coming in His kingdom;" in John 21:22, "If I will that he" (John) "tarry till I come, what is *that* to thee?" which is a clear intimation that John should live till Christ came; *i.e.,* till the destruction of Jerusalem, A.D. 70; in Luke 10:12, "That it shall be more tolerable in *that* day" (meaning the day of His coming, when He would judge them), "than for that city;" in verse 35, "To keep their lights burning;" in Luke 12:36, "To act like men that wait for their Lord; that when He cometh and knocketh, they may open unto Him immediately;" in verse 40, "Be ye also ready, for the Son of man cometh at an hour when ye think not;" in verse 56, addressing the people, "Ye hypocrites! ye can discern the face of the sky and of the earth, but how is it that ye discern not *this* time?" (thereby meaning the time of *their* judgment at His coming, then close at hand); in Matthew 26:29, He says He shall not drink again of the "fruit of the vine" till He drinks it with His disciples in His Father's kingdom; in Matthew 24:34, "Verily, I say unto you, *this* generation" (by the words "this generation" Christ always means His contemporaries) "shall not pass till all these things" (meaning the destruction of Jerusalem, which occurred A.D. 70, and the tribulation preceding it and His second coming) "be fulfilled." "Heaven and earth," Christ adds with terrible emphasis (verse 35), "shall pass away, but my words shall *not* pass away;" and therefore, we conclude, He came at the destruction of Jerusalem, A.D. 70, "in the clouds of Heaven, with power and great glory;" *i.e.,* within the generation of his contemporaries.

In the 14th, 15th, 16th, and 17th chapters of John (he alone records it), Christ discourses tenderly to His disciples (not to the world) as He is about to leave them and return to the bosom of the Father. Among other cheering things He tells them, "In my Father's house are many mansions. If it *were* not so, I would have told you. I go to prepare a place for you; and if I go and prepare a place for you, I will come again, and receive you unto myself, that where I *am, there* ye may be also." (John 14:2-3). "I will not leave you comfortless; I will come to you. Yet a little while and the world seeth me no more; but ye see me; because I live ye shall live also. At that day" (meaning the day of his coming), "ye shall know that I *am* in my Father, and ye in me, and I in you." (John 14:18-20). "Ye have heard how I said unto you, I go away and come *again* unto you." (John 14:28).

The above words of Christ are the foundation for the hope which has existed in the Christian Church since His ascension, that some time He would "come again" to earth. And we are here to show that He *did* come at the destruction of Jerusalem, A.D. 70. He came exactly as He said He would, and as the primitive Christians expected, and yet, for eighteen centuries, Christendom has known it not. Further on we shall show why they have not known it.

The locality of Christ's coming was "in the clouds of heaven," directly over Jerusalem; *i.e.,* at the place of His greatest earthly agony. At His first coming He was crucified at Jerusalem amid the scoffs of the world. At His second coming He stood over Jerusalem, in the clouds of heaven with power and great glory, "judging the quick and dead."

We ascertain the *time* of Christ's coming thus: "Immediately after the tribulation of those days"—*i.e* immediately after the destruction of Jerusalem and the tribulation preceding it, says Christ (Matt. 24:29-31), "shall the sun be darkened, and the moon shall not give her light, and the stars shall fall from heaven, and the powers of the heavens shall be shaken; and *then* shall appear the sign of the Son of man in heaven, and *then* shall all the tribes of the earth mourn, and *they*"—*i.e.,* the tribes (see Rev. 1:7)—"shall see the Son of man coming in the clouds of heaven with power and great glory. And He shall send His angels with a great sound of a trumpet, and they shall gather together His elect from the four winds, from one end of the heaven to the other." Again he says (Matt. 24:33), "When ye shall see all these things," meaning the desolation of Jerusalem and the tribulation preceding it, "know that it" *i.e.,* My coming "is near, even at the door." Again, He says (Luke 21:20), "When ye shall see Jerusalem compassed with armies, *then* know that the desolation thereof is nigh," *i.e.,* that Jerusalem is about to be destroyed, and my words concerning it fulfilled, "and when these things (He continues in verse 28) begin to come to pass, then, look up and lift up your heads, for your redemption draweth nigh," *i.e.,* that I am about to come and take you with me to glory. And, therefore, we conclude: (1) that the destruction of Jerusalem; (2) the coming of Christ; and (3) as the consequence of His coming, the "redemption" of His disciples, to whom He was speaking, were simultaneous events.

In the 24th of Matthew, Christ predicts the occurrence of

certain events before His coming, which we now examine, and thereby show that every prediction He made relating to His coming was fulfilled prior to the destruction of Jerusalem; *i.e.,* prior to His coming.

In Matthew 24:2, Christ says, "See ye not all these things? Verily, I say unto you there shall not be left standing here" (meaning the temple) "one stone upon another that shall not be thrown down."

History records the destruction of Jerusalem and the temple thus: "In A.D. 66" (American Encyclopaedia, vol. 10, page 2) "the Jews, goaded to despair by the tyranny of the Romans, revolted, took possession of the city, and a Roman army, commanded by Certius Gallus, governor of Syria, was routed in battle before its walls." Titus, son of the emperor, Vespasian, regained it in A.D. 70, after one of the most terrible battles on record. His troops, maddened by the resistance of the defenders, spared neither age nor sex. Thousands of Jews, seeing all hope lost, threw themselves headlong from the towers, and a horrible scene of carnage ensued. According to Josephus, over eleven hundred thousand Jews perished in the siege, and ninety-seven thousand were carried into captivity. Titus himself was unable to control the rage of his troops, and with regret saw the temple (which he had intended to preserve as a memorial of his own victory) burned and the entire city razed to the ground; and thus Christ's prediction, made A.D. 33, or shortly before His crucifixion, was literally fulfilled. Everything he foretold concerning the temple, city, and people of the Jews was fulfilled in the most astonishing manner. It was witnessed by Josephus, a Jewish contemporary of Christ, and who is acknowledged to be a historian of indisputable veracity on all those transactions concerning the destruction of Jerusalem. The wars and rumors of war, the Antichrists, the famines, the pestilences, the earthquakes, the "great tribulation," etc. spoken of by the evangelists as events preceding Christ's coming, *all* came to pass prior to the destruction of Jerusalem. Josephus records the occurrence of these great events as a matter of history of which he was an eye-witness; but he knew nothing of the scripture containing Christ's prophecy. He speaks contemptuously of Christ, as "one Jesus, a country fellow, who went about crying with a loud voice, 'Woe, woe, to the city, to the people, and to the temple.'" The whole land of Judea is represented at that time "as a woman in grievous travail." Christ himself said upon *that* generation (meaning his contemporaries) should "come *all* the righteous blood shed upon earth." "Verily, I say unto you, all these things shall come upon this generation." (Matt. 23:35-36). And it did come. Christ's contemporaries crucified God's only Son, and, therefore, the Almighty cursed them by sending upon them "such tribulation as was not since the beginning of the world, no, nor ever shall be." (Matt. 24:21). All this would immediately precede Christ's coming, and therefore we conclude He came immediately *after* these events—*i.e.,* at the destruction of Jerusalem, A.D. 70.

In Matthew 24:14, Christ says, "The gospel must be preached to all the world," (meaning as it existed in his day) "for a witness unto all nations, and then shall the end come." (Not the end of the world, but of the Primitive Church and Jewish nation. They were judged, both quick and dead, at Christ's coming).

Paul records the universal publication of the gospel thus: Rom. 1:8, "Your faith is spoken of throughout the whole world," (meaning the world as it existed in his day). Rom. 10:18, Your faith is spoken of "unto the ends of the world." Rom. 16:26, "That he had made known the Gospel to all nations." Col. 1:23, That the Gospel was "preached to every creature under heaven," whereof he was a minister. I Thess. 1:8, "Your faith is spoken of in every place." II Thess. 1:3, "Your faith groweth exceedingly." II Tim. 4:17, That he had preached the Gospel unto "all the Gentiles." And therefore, on the words of Jesus Christ that the end should come immediately *after* the universal publication of the Gospel, we conclude the end did come—*i.e.,* the end of the primitive Church and Jewish nation, which He judged at His second coming.

The coming of Antichrist is predicted before Christ's coming, in Matt. 24:5, 11, 24; in II Thess. 2:3; in II Tim. 3:1-9. 13; in II Pet. 2:1-2; in II Pet. 2:3-4; in I John 4:1, and Jude 18-19. In I John 2:18-19, 22, and I John 4:3, we are told that Antichrist has

28

come, whereby "we know it is the last time," thereby meaning that John and his contemporaries knew they were on the verge of Christ's coming, because the appearance of Antichrist was the *sure* sign that Christ would speedily appear. John wrote about A.D. 69, or a year before the destruction of Jerusalem.

"Behold, he cometh with clouds," (Rev. 1:7) "and every eye shall see Him, and they also which pierced Him, and all kindreds of the earth shall wail because of Him." Christ, at His first coming, was crucified at Jerusalem amid the scoffs of the world. At His second coming He stood over Jerusalem "in the clouds of heaven," judging "the quick and dead," (see II Tim. 4:1-3), and they, *i.e.,* "the quick and dead," *did* see His coming "with power and great glory." "For as the lightning cometh out of the east," says Christ (Matt. 24:27), "and shineth even unto the west," *so* shall the coming of the Son of Man be, *i.e.,* it was an *instantaneous event* "in the clouds of heaven." He came "with His mighty angels," (see II Thes. 1:7-10), like a thief at night, snatched the righteous part of the primitive Church, and the righteous dead of past ages, and hurried with them into glory. Perhaps the memory of His sufferings here below haunted Him, and He tarried not! He came like a mighty rushing wind, judged the wicked, took His own, and back He went to the bosom of the Father.

This was the first resurrection and first judgment, corresponding to the Jewish and Gentile dispensations. The Jews, as a nation, had their judgment at the destruction of Jerusalem, and the Gentiles will have theirs at the end of the world.

Peter's idea (II Pet. 3:10-12), that Christ's coming and the "burning up" of this physical universe are simultaneous events, (and that is the popular idea about Christ's coming), we are obliged to reject, in view of his record, as uninspired. He alone had that idea. Christ and Paul and John taught it not. And yet, even Peter expected the coming of Christ within the lifetime of his contemporaries. In I Pet. 4:7, he says, "The end of all things is at hand," *i.e.,* I expect the speedy coming of Christ; in II Pet. 1:16, he speaks of the "coming of our Lord Jesus Christ;" in II Pet. 3:10, "the day of the Lord will come as a thief in the night;" in II Pet. 3:12, "looking for and hastening unto the coming of the day of God."

We live eighteen hundred years after Peter, and this globe has not burned yet. And therefore we conclude his idea that Christ's coming, and the burning up of this earth are simultaneous events, savors of the things of man, and not of God. Peter was a bold, impulsive, unlearned man. In many things "he was to be blamed." Paul "withstood him to the face" Peter "rebuked" the Master. No other disciple had the impudence to do that. He thrice solemnly denied the son of Man in the darkest hour of his life on earth! In Luke 22:31-32, Christ says to Peter, "Behold, Satan hath desired to have you, but I have prayed for thee that thy faith fail not. When thou art converted, strengthen thy brethren." In Eph. 2:7, Paul says, "That in the ages to come He (i.e., God) might show the exceeding riches of His grace in His kindness toward us through Christ Jesus," which opposes Peter's idea that the "burning up of the earth," and Christ's coming (which he himself believed was at hand when on earth) are simultaneous events. We believe [that] Peter's idea—that Christ's coming and the destruction of this physical universe are simultaneous events— has darkened the mind of Christendom these eighteen centuries, touching His coming, more than anything in the Bible. If Christ and Paul had had such an idea, they would have stated it. For eighteen centuries Christendom has argued thus: "In II Pet. 3:10-12, it is said Christ's coming and the 'burning up' of the earth are simultaneous events. The earth has not burned yet; therefore, Christ has not yet come. Therefore, we expect Him, and Christendom for eighteen centuries has expected Him"—in vain. He never has come (save as herein stated), and never will. God wanted to curse the Antichrist part of the primitive Church on account of their unbelief concerning the coming of Christ then at hand, and therefore allowed Peter's idea to go into the Bible. See II Thess. 2:11.

Paul's expectations concerning Christ's coming we gather thus: Rom. 13:11, "It is high time to awake out of sleep; for now is our salvation nearer than when we believed;" Rom. 13:12, "The night is far spent, the day is at hand;" I Cor. 1:7, "Waiting for the coming of our Lord Jesus Christ;" I Cor. 1:8, "That ye may be blameless in the day of our Lord Jesus Christ;" I Cor. 4:5, "Judge nothing, before the time, until the Lord come;" I Cor. 7:29, "The time is short," (i.e., I expect the speedy coming of Christ;) I Cor. 13:12, "Now we see through a glass, darkly; but then" (referring to Christ's coming), "face to face;" I Cor. 15:51, "We shall not all sleep," (meaning thereby that some of Paul's contemporaries would live till Christ came, i.e., until the destruction of Jerusalem, A.D. 70); II Cor. 1:14, bespeaks of their rejoicing in "the day of our Lord Jesus;" Phil. 1:6, "He which hath begun a good work in you will perform it until the day of Jesus Christ;" Phil. 1:10, "they are to be without offence till the day of Christ;" Phil. 2:16, "That I may rejoice in the day of Christ;" Phil. 3:20, "For our conversation is in heaven, from whence also we look for the Savior, the Lord Jesus Christ;" Phil. 4:5, "The Lord is at hand;" Col. 3:4, "When Christ, who is life, shall appear, then shall ye also appear with him in glory;" I Thess. 1:10, he exhorts them to "wait for God's Son from heaven;" I Thess. 2:19, "Are not even ye in the presence of our Lord Jesus Christ at His coming?" I Thess. 3:13, he speaks of their hearts being established "in holiness before God, even our Father, at the coining of our Lord Jesus Christ with all His saints;" I Thess. 4:15-17. he says, "We which are alive and remain unto the coming of the Lord shall be caught up together with them (meaning the 'dead in Christ') in the clouds to meet the Lord in the air; and so shall we ever be with the Lord;" I Thess. 5:2, "The day of the Lord so cometh as a thief in the night;" I Thess. 5:4, "But ye brethren are not in darkness, that that day should overtake you as a thief;" I Thess. 5:6, "Therefore, let us watch and be sober;" I Thess. 5:23, "I pray God your whole spirit and soul and body be preserved blameless unto the coming of our Lord Jesus Christ;" II Thess. 1:7-9, he says that the "Lord Jesus shall be revealed from heaven with His mighty angels, in flaming fire, taking vengeance on them that know not God and obey not the Gospel of our Lord Jesus Christ, who shall punish them with everlasting destruction from the presence of the Lord and from the glory of His power;" II Thess. 1:10, he speaks of Christ's coining to be glorified in "His saints, and to be admired in all them that believe in that day;" thereby meaning the day

31

of Christ's coming, which occurred at the destruction of Jerusalem, A.D. 70, when He judged the primitive Church and Jewish nation. In II Thess. 2:1-3, he exhorts them "not to be soon shaken in mind" on account of the speedy coming "of our Lord Jesus Christ," and says, "that that day" (meaning the day of His coming) shall not come until the "man of sin be revealed." In verse 7 we are told that the mystery of iniquity (*i.e.,* "the man of sin") doth already work. In II John 2:18, and 4:3, we again have the fulfilment of Paul's prediction concerning the appearance of Antichrist before Christ's coming. II Thess. 3:5, "The Lord direct your hearts into the love of God, and into the patient waiting for Christ." I Tim. 6:14, "That thou keep this commandment without spot, unrebukable, until the appearing of our Lord Jesus Christ;" II Tim. 1:10, he speaks of the "appearing of our Savior Jesus Christ;" II Tim.1:18, "The Lord grant unto him (Onesiphorus) that he may find mercy of the Lord in that day" (meaning the day of Christ's coming) "for he oft refreshed me, and was not ashamed of my chains." In II Tim. 4:13, Paul says, "That Jesus Christ shall judge the quick and the dead at His appearing," and exhorts Timothy "to preach the word in season and out of season," for the "time would come when they would not endure sound doctrine, but after their own lusts follow deceitful teachers having itching ears that they should turn away their ears from the truth, and "be turned unto fables" (thereby meaning that Antichrist was abroad, which was a *sure* sign that Christ would speedily appear). II Tim. 4:8, he speaks of a "crown of righteousness" which Christ would give Him at His coming, and to them also "who love His appearing." Titus 2:13, "Looking for that blessed hope, and the glorious appearing of the great God and our Savior Jesus Christ." Heb. 10:37. "For yet a little while, and He that shall come, *will come*, and will not tarry."

James's expectations we gather thus: James 5:7, "Be patient, therefore, brethren, unto the coming of the Lord." James 5:8, "Be ye also patient; establish your hearts; for the coming of the Lord draweth nigh." James 5:9, "Behold, the Judge standeth before the door."

John wrote in the very last days of the primitive Church,

and we gather his expectations thus: I John 2:18, "Little children (how tenderly he speaks), it is the last time (as Christ is about to appear and take us with Him to glory), and as ye have heard that Antichrist shall come, even now are there many Antichrists, whereby we know it is the last time." I John 2:28, "And now, little children, abide in Him, that when He shall appear we may have confidence, and not be ashamed before Him at His coming." I John 3:2, "Beloved, now are we the sons of God, and it doth not yet appear what we shall be; but we know that when He shall appear, we shall be like Him." I John 3:19, "We are of the truth, and shall assure our hearts before Him."

Jude's expectations we gather thus: Verses 14 and 15, "Behold, the Lord cometh with ten thousand of His saints to execute judgment upon all." Verse 21, "Keep yourselves in the love of God, looking for the mercy of our Lord Jesus Christ unto eternal life."

We now examine the book of Revelation concerning Christ's second coming. In Rev. 1:1, we are told the things therein mentioned "must shortly come to pass;" in verse 2, "The time is at hand;" in verse 7, "Behold, He cometh with clouds, and every eye shall see Him, and they also which pierced Him, and all kindred of the earth shall wail because of Him." In verse 11 Jesus Christ says, "I am Alpha and Omega, the first and the last;" in verse 18, "I am He that liveth and was dead; and behold, I am alive forevermore, and have the keys of hell and of death;" in Rev. 2:5, "Repent, or I will come unto thee quickly;" in verse 16, "Repent, or I will come unto thee quickly;" in verse 25, "That which ye have already, hold fast till I come;" in Rev. 3:3, "Hold fast and repent," "If thou shall not watch, I will come on thee as a thief;" in verse 11, "Behold, I come quickly; hold fast what thou hast, that no man take thy crown;" in verse 20, "Behold I stand at the door and knock;" in Rev. 13:14, "The second woe is past, and behold, the third one cometh quickly;" in Rev. 14:7, "Fear God and give glory to Him, for the hour of judgment is come;" "and worship Him that made heaven and earth, and the sea and the fountains of waters;" in verse 15, "Thrust in thy sickle and reap, for the time is come for thee to reap;" in Rev. 16:15, "Behold I come as a thief;" in Rev. 19:7, "The marriage of the Lamb is come;" in Rev. 22:6, He speaks of things which "must shortly be done;" in verse 7, "Behold, I come quickly;" in verse 10, "The time is at hand;" in verse 12, "Behold, I come quickly to reward every man according as his work shall be;" in verse 13, "I am Alpha and Omega, the beginning and the end, the first and the last." The very last words Jesus Christ says in the Bible are, (Rev. 22:20), "Surely I come quickly. Even so." Says John, "Come, Lord Jesus."

We have now examined every verse in the New Testament touching Christ's second coming. Can any rational mind doubt but Jesus Christ *said* He would "come again" within the lifetime of his contemporaries; that Paul and the leaders of the Primitive Church expected Him, and that, as a matter of fact, He *did* come at the destruction of Jerusalem, A.D. 70, "in the clouds of heaven, with power and great glory," and judge the entire race, except those *then* living on earth; (and even soon some of these were taken).

In the interest of a sound theology it is of the utmost importance to know the truth about Christ's second coming. It is useless for Christendom to hope and pray for His coming, because it is a fact already accomplished. They may as well look it square in the face and adapt their faith and conduct to the fact. It is believed these views are destined to revolutionize the theology of eighteen centuries. Christendom must have a *new* theology— a theology to fit the fact that Christ came in A.D. 70.

The great practical effect of this doctrine will be to establish the faith of Christendom in the Bible. This doctrine throws a calcium light upon the New Testament. It illuminates its otherwise mysterious words, verses, and chapters. No one can understand the Bible without *this* view of the second coming. It is a living stream of water running through the New Testament. This doctrine is the missing link, uniting Primitive Christianity with modern Christianity, and, it is believed, Holy Ghost power will come to the church by a belief in this doctrine. Thousands have rejected the Bible, to their eternal death, on account of its apparent inconsistency, not knowing the truth concerning Christ's second coming.

This doctrine *ends* the communion: "Do this," says Christ, "in remembrance of me, *till* I come." If we behold His coming eighteen centuries in the past, an ordinance commemorating Him as a conquering hero would be appropriate.

A correct knowledge of Christ's second coming is almost as important as a knowledge of His first coming. At His first coming He was crucified at Jerusalem amid the scoffs of the world. At His second coming He was a conquering hero. He *then* stood over Jerusalem "in the clouds of heaven," judging the "quick and dead."

Judgment, says Paul, comes first to the Jews; then to the Gentiles. At Christ's second coming God not only judged the entire human race, except those *then* on earth, but He especially judged the Jewish nation, destroying its nationality. For two thousand years, *i.e.,* since God's covenant with Abraham, He had sent upon the Jewish nation the rain and sunshine of religious discipline, and the harvest was reaped at Christ's second coming. For nearly two thousand years, *i.e.,* since Christ came, A.D. 70, the Gentiles have been under God's care, and the Gentile harvest must now be near at hand. We believe we are living in "the dispensation of the fullness of times" (Eph. 1:10; Rom. 11:25); that the second resurrection and final judgment are in the near future, which will end the Gentile harvest.

At the final judgment Christ will judge the world from His throne in heaven, and He has no need to return to earth for any purpose. It is not necessary, or even desirable, that Christ should return to earth again.

When He was here He was badly treated. Heaven is a thousand times better than this sin-cursed earth. We submit, that our friends of the Prophetic Conference are in the dark, and we offer them this book, as the only rational solution of this matter.

We epitomize the history of the race thus: Adam, Noah, Abraham, Christ's birth, Christ's death and resurrection, Christ's second coming, A.D. 70. Christ's second coming is the pivotal fact of history. Standing on it we gaze up and down the ages. We look back to Adam, and forward to the present. Hereafter we shall review history, standing on Christ's coming A.D. 70, as the greatest fact of history.

In conclusion, men like John the Baptist, Paul the Apostle, Luther, Calvin, Knox, Wesley, have been the world's reformers. Every one of them was a reformer, because he was a theologian who believed, and preached, and fought for the pure doctrines of the Word of God.

CHRISTIANITY REVIEWED SINCE A.D. 70.

This was written in August and September, 1878.

IN the last section we showed that Christ came for the second time at the destruction of Jerusalem, A.D. 70; that he then judged the entire race, except those on earth at the moment of His appearing at the siege of Jerusalem; and that the preaching of Paul and the other apostles was a preparation for their judgment at that second coining. We also showed that Jerusalem was destroyed A.D. 70, by Titus, a Roman general, and that the "wars and rumors of wars," the Antichrists, the famines, the pestilences, the earthquakes, the great tribulations, the universal publication of the Gospel, etc. spoken of by the Evangelists as *events* preceding Christ's coming, *all* came to pass prior to His coming, *i.e.,* prior to the destruction of Jerusalem.

We now propose to review Christianity on the basis of Christ's second coming, at the destruction of Jerusalem, A.D. 70.

Josephus, and other historians, make no mention of Christ's appearing at the destruction of Jerusalem, because it was an event "in the clouds of heaven" directly over Jerusalem.

At the time Jerusalem was destroyed most of Christ's followers had gone within the vail. Over eleven hundred thousand Jews perished at the siege of Jerusalem, and the abduction of a few despised individuals at such a time of carnage would attract no attention. Josephus and the historians were too busy recording what happened on earth to record what happened "in the clouds of heaven." Besides, how could Josephus *see* what was going on "in the clouds?" "The world seeth me no more," said Christ, with special reference to His second coming. His coming in judgment was an event in the *spiritual,* and not in the natural world. His appearing "in the clouds of heaven," at the destruction of Jerusalem, and the slaughter of eleven hundred thousand Jews, was the outward sign of that spiritual judgment, in which the Almighty judged the entire race, except those living on earth at the destruction of Jerusalem. All who had lived on the earth, and died, were judged at Christ's second coming, at the siege of Jerusalem, A.D. 70.

There were two classes in the Primitive Church—those that expected Christ's coming and those that did not. An individual's belief or disbelief in His coming decided His final destiny. He appeared at the siege of Jerusalem "with His mighty angels," to those who were looking for Him, and took them to glory. To those who looked *not for* Him He came not. *They* were left on earth, and *their* seed has represented Christianity all these ages. *They* were the unfaithful servants of whom Christ so often spake.

On nearly every page of the New Testament, we find the speedy coming of Christ "in the clouds of heaven with power and great glory," held up by the Evangelists, and especially by the Apostle Paul, as an event which would give to the "saints" of the Primitive Church, and the righteous dead of past ages, a secure and glorious redemption. It was the consummation of their effort, the reward of their faith and devotion to the Master; and yet, for eighteen centuries, Christendom has known it not.

The very curse Paul says (II Thess. 2:11) should come upon the church, has been upon it since Christ came, A. D. 70. "And for this cause," says Paul (thereby meaning the unbelief of the Antichrist part of the Primitive Church, concerning Christ's coming, then close at hand), "God shall send them," (meaning the Antichrist part of the Primitive Church, and which Christianity since has represented), "strong delusion," that they should "believe a lie;" and Christendom, for eighteen centuries, has not known the truth touching Christ's second coming. The reason they have not known it, is because it was the *Antichrist* part of the Primitive Church which Christ left on earth when He judged the race at the siege of Jerusalem. It is *this* apostate Christianity that has assumed to represent Christ all these ages. As they forsook the coming of the Lord, so has the church, commonly called Christian, done in all ages. The Christianity of Paul's church was wonderfully different in spirituality and Holy Ghost power from any church since his time.

As we read the history of this apostate Christianity, we are appalled at the record. And herein we find an unanswerable confirmation of our doctrine of Christ's second coming. Our doctrine shows that Christ's second coming *occurred* at the siege of Jerusalem, A.D. 70; that he then took the "saints" of the Primitive Church, and the righteous dead of past ages to glory, *and left the unrighteous part of said church;* and that this fact accounts for the terrible record of Christianity during the "dark ages." At that time, Christ transferred *His* interest in the church which He founded, from earth to heaven, and He is in no way responsible for the doings of the apostate part of that church since. It is a terrible libel on Christ to make Him in any way responsible for the iniquity of that apostate Church during the "dark ages." It was this Apostate Church that Martin Luther and his associates sought to reform.

We now propose to glance briefly through the record of this Apostate Church, to the end, that we may show the wickedness of its pretensions.

From the siege of Jerusalem to Martin Luther, covers a period of fifteen long and weary centuries. During these "dark ages" the Almighty seems to have withdrawn all interest in human affairs. Nothing can equal the ignorance, superstition and licentiousness of *that* time. In the so-called Christian Church, and out of it, iniquity was rampant. Many volumes have been written portraying the horrors of this dark period of the world's history; but it is not our purpose now to enter into the details of that polluted period. We desire only to present a general view of the world during the fifteen centuries preceding the coming of Martin Luther, to the end, we may appreciate the work he and his associates accomplished daring the reformation of the sixteenth century.

After a time the apostates whom Christ *left on earth* grew mighty, and assumed by His authority full power over the body, soul, and estate of their deluded victims. They propagated this fanaticism with so much success that vast multitudes adhered to them, and they were known as the Church of Rome. The ringleader of this delusion was called a Pontiff. In time, he and his cardinals, bishops, and underlings, grew rich and all-powerful. They claimed to be the visible representatives of the "dear Lord" on earth, and to have the keys of heaven and hell, and to do all things by His authority. In the course of a few centuries, these apostates *grew* immensely rich and correspondingly sensual and corrupt. The worst thing about it was, that they should carry on their iniquity in the name of "the meek and lowly Jesus," who had not where to "lay His head" while He tarried here below.

About the commencement of the sixteenth century these lordly Pontiffs became so corrupt and oppressive that the people demanded a reform, and Mr. Martin Luther, a poor and obscure monk, offered his service.

It is almost impossible for us of the nineteenth century to realize the horrible superstition, fanaticism, and licentiousness which oppressed the people at the commencement of the sixteenth century. When the time came, in the Providence of God, for Luther to strike these corrupt Pontiffs, he struck them with tremendous power. He even startled himself, but he dare not draw back. He stuck close to God, the Father, and He helped him through.

The powers and emoluments of the Pontiff at this time were almost incredible. He had his emissaries all over his dominions, gathering "lucre" into his treasury, that he and his co-scoundrels might live in gorgeous palaces, surrounded by luxury and lust. He claimed, and the people believed, he had Divine authority to grant *indulgence* to commit the most horrible crimes, and to gratify the most lustful propensities. He sent one Tetzel into Saxony, the home of Luther, to sell these indulgences, and this brazen fellow aroused Luther's indignation, and set him to thinking. This thinking was the beginning of a reformation which set all Germany in motion, and proved of incalculable value to the race.

It was a bold thing for Martin Luther to strike the Roman Pontiff. In doing it he pierced the tradition and wisdom of fifteen centuries. During all this time the Pontiffs had been growing rich and mighty, and it seemed like madness for a poor and obscure monk to oppose them. For three years Luther stood alone. "Not a soul," he says, "for three years extended the hand of fellowship." After that his views began to prevail, and then, "every one," he says, "wanted to share in the triumph." Little by little, the best minds of Germany surrounded Luther, and thereafter success was established. Germany had long groaned under the spiritual despotism of the Roman Pontiff, and it was ripe for a reformation.

Luther was God's man for this reformation. His genius was

truly great; his memory vast and tenacious; his patience incredible; his magnanimity invincible and unshaken by the vicissitudes of human affairs; and his learning most extensive for the age in which he lived.

From this reformation came the Evangelical or Lutheran Church, so named in honor of its founder, Martin Luther, who sought to restore to its native lustre the Gospel of Christ, which had been for ages covered with the darkness of superstition. His followers were moved to call the new church *Lutheran*, in response to a natural sentiment of gratitude to him by whose ministry the clouds of superstition had been chiefly dispelled, and who had pointed out to them the "Son of God as the only proper object of trust to miserable mortals."

The rise of the Lutheran Church dates from that remarkable period when Pope Leo X drove Luther and his friends from the bosom of the Roman hierarchy, by a solemn and violent sentence of excommunication. From that time it has gradually assumed the dignity of a lawful and complete church, totally independent of the laws and jurisdiction of the Roman Pontiffs

The leading doctrine of the Lutheran Church was that the Scriptures are the "infallible rule of faith and practice."

It was the work of Luther and his associates to rescue the Bible from the Roman Pontiffs. The Bible was exceedingly scarce at that time, and the few copies extant were kept under lock and key by the Pontiffs. Luther translated the Bible into German. He also inundated Germany with pamphlets on Biblical subjects. His great doctrine was *"Justifcation by faith in Christ."* He set the people to studying the Word of God. The more they examined it, the less power the Pontiffs had over them. Little by little their power was gone; not only in Germany, but in England, Ireland, Spain, Italy, and France—in fact, wherever their spiritual dominions extended.

Next to Luther, as a reformer, stood Philip Melancthon.

After Luther's death, which happened in 1546, at the age of 63, Melancthon became head of the Lutheran Church. He was a man of different stamp from Luther. Not so vehement, but more learned. His genius and culture were extraordinary. He differed with Luther on some important points, but otherwise they were in full sympathy. He was of the opinion that many things in the Roman Church might be tolerated, which Luther considered as absolutely insupportable. This diversity of views, after Luther's death, created internal dissensions in the church, and caused much trouble.

If our doctrine, to wit, that Christ's second coming *occurred* at the siege of Jerusalem, A.D. 70, had been known to Luther and his associates, it would have saved them a vast deal of trouble, and many long and wearisome and useless controversies. So with all the great churchmen of the past. They all missed the truth which it has pleased God, the Father, to reveal through us. The church records are full of controversies touching the Lord's Supper, the communion, etc. all subjects relating to Christ's second coming.

Christ said, "Do this," to wit, the Lord's Supper, **"till I come, in remembrance of me."** This holds good *only* till He comes. The church all these ages has not known of His coming at the siege of Jerusalem, A.D. 70, and consequently has been taught to expect Him, and to commemorate His coming by the sacrament of the "Lord's Supper." Whereas, in fact and in truth, He came at the destruction of Jerusalem A.D. 70, and therefore, the exhortation to "do this" (to wit, the Lord's Supper), "till I come," is wholly irrelevant.

Christ, at His first coming, was crucified at Jerusalem amid the scoffs of the world. At His second coming He was a conquering hero. He then stood over Jerusalem, in the "clouds of heaven" judging "the quick and dead;" and therefore, an ordinance commemorating Him as a **conquering** hero, is only appropriate.

Since the Reformation Christianity has been divided and subdivided and redivided, into the thousand and one isms that curse it today. Notwithstanding this, Christianity has done great good, and we are profoundly thankful for what it has accomplished. Its ascent out of the pollution and superstition of the "dark ages" has been accomplished little by little, and by painful effort. The Christianity of today represents the faith and tears and conflicts of the Fathers. From time to time they have appeared with new light, propelling it onward and upward.

We now propose to interview some of these Fathers. And first comes John Calvin. He had some new ideas. From him came Presbyterianism.

As we glance through the records of church history since the Reformation, we are astonished at the trouble and dissensions the Fathers have had from not knowing the *truth* about Christ's second coming. It has caused them more trouble than anything else. The greatest and wisest men in the church for eighteen centuries have not understood Christ's saying: "If I will that he (John) tarry till I come, what is *that* to thee?" This refers to Christ's coming within the lifetime of his contemporaries, to wit, at the destruction of Jerusalem, A.D. 70. The church Fathers have given it all sorts of interpretations except the true one. Not even our keen friend, Mr. Calvin, saw it.

The Presbyterians of this age are so eminently respectable that we shall trespass upon our time somewhat to give a condensed view of the great work of their founder, John Calvin. Calvin was born in 1509, and was bred to the law. As a student his success was "most rapid and amazing." He acquired the knowledge of religion by a diligent perusal of the Scriptures, and early saw the necessity of "reforming the established system of doctrine and worship." His zeal exposed to him various perils, and his connection with the friends of the Reformation, who were frequently committed to the flames, placed him more than once in imminent danger; but out of it all he was delivered.

Calvin had some new ideas concerning the decrees of God, respecting the eternal condition of men, and they stirred the people immensely. He maintained that the everlasting condition of mankind in the future world was determined from all eternity by the unchangeable order of the Deity, and that this absolute determination of His will and good pleasure was the only source of happiness or misery to every individual. He propagated his opinion by his writings, and by public discussions, and by the "ministry of his disciples." In time it was inserted in the national creeds, and "thus made a public article of faith."

Although in sympathy with Luther and the work of reformation, Calvin had some ideas of his own, and he pushed out for himself. He now had a large following, and they were known as the Reformed Church. He settled at Geneva, in Switzerland, where he acquired the greatest reputation and authority. He surpassed all the divines of his age in laborious application, force of eloquence, and extent of genius. He was the head of the Reformed Church in Geneva, and also acquired great influence in the political administration of that republic. His views and projects were grand and extensive. He not only undertook to give strength and vigor to the rising church, by strict discipline, but proposed to render Geneva the mother of all Reformed Churches, as Wittenberg was of all Lutheran Churches. He proposed to establish a theological seminary for the instruction of ministers, who were to propagate the Protestant cause through the most distant nations. He proposed to render the government, discipline, and doctrine of Geneva the model to be followed by all the Reformed Churches in the world; and he in great part succeeded in the execution of this grand scheme. His fame and learning induced many persons of rank and fortune to settle at Geneva. Many others came out of curiosity to bear the discourses which he delivered in public. Studious youths came from all parts to the Geneva University, and its fame extended everywhere. By this means Calvin propagated his doctrine all through Europe. In the midst of this activity he died in the year 1564.

In August, 1878, there met in this very city of Geneva, in a hall dedicated to Calvin, the International Convention of Young Men's Christian Associations. They came from the Protestant churches of all lands to confer as to the best methods of pushing the Master's work. I wonder what Calvin would have said if he could have spoken to them, assembled, as they were, in his old home at Geneva. Methinks he would have seen the travail of his soul and wept for joy.

In these latter days these Christian Associations have done a vast work in rescuing souls from perdition. About forty years ago the first one was established in London, England, by Mr. George Williams, a retired merchant. (He was present and took an active part at the Geneva Conference). Since then they have multiplied in all directions. At this moment there are two thousand of these associations in different parts of the world. May God bless them and their workers.

HADES AND THE FINAL JUDGMENT

This was written in January, 1878.

WHEN Christ appeared at the destruction of Jerusalem, A.D. 70, the entire human race (save those then living on earth) were judged; *i.e.,* the "sheep" were separated from the "goats;" *i.e.,* the righteous went to heaven and the wicked to eternal punishment. Prior to this resurrection and judgment, the entire human race (*i.e.,* the dead part of it) were in Hades, awaiting their resurrection and judgment, which took place when Christ appeared at the destruction of Jerusalem.

What kind of a place is Hades? We answer, Hades is the resting-place of the dead. It is the place where the dead (both righteous and wicked) await their final disposition, the righteous being detained for heaven, and the wicked for eternal punishment.

The Bible characterizes the inhabitants of Hades as in a state of *sleep* (Dan. 12:2; I Cor. 15:51), but they are not in a state of absolute unconsciousness. They are simply withdrawn from the world of sense, like a person in ordinary slumber. They are in the *soul* of the universe instead of the *body.* Their operation on the surface ceases at death. Their sleep is opposed to the visible activity of this world, and also to the perfect activity of the resurrection world. After Christ's crucifixion He remained in Hades three days, and then He ascended to the Father. Before He ascended He appeared to His disciples and said, "All power is given to me, in heaven and on earth," *i.e.,* He entered upon a career of activity in both worlds. The saints in Hades sleep until their resurrection, when they, too, will be active in both worlds. The "saints" are said to "sleep in the dust of the earth," because *their* abode is not in heaven, but in Hades; *i.e.,* until their resurrection.

Hades and mortality (*i.e.,* this world) may be compared to two apartments on the same floor of a house. Heaven, or God's home, is the floor above. The resurrection is a transit to God's home. It is not a transit from one apartment to another. Enoch and Elijah passed into Hades by translation. And Lazarus returned from Hades at the call of Christ. Christ ascended out of Hades at the call of God. This same mighty power will at last draw "all men to Christ," (John 12:32), the righteous as well as the wicked. The dead, small and great, must stand before God.

The *Paradise of Hades* is not the final abode of the righteous. They are to be brought up for judgment and then pass into the kingdom of the Father. Hades is not the final abode of the wicked. They, too, must appear before the judgment-seat of Christ, and then pass into the lake of fire which burns for ever and ever. (Rev. 20:10-15; and 21:8).

As the entire human race *(i.e.,* the dead part of it) prior to the destruction of Jerusalem, A.D. 70, were detained in Hades, awaiting their resurrection and judgment, so the inhabitants of this earth, since A.D. 70, have been detained in Hades awaiting their resurrection and judgment, which will take place at the end of the world.

Paul (he was executed A.D. 68) only waited two years in the Paradise of Hades after his death for his "crown," *i.e.,* till Christ came, A.D. 70. Abraham, however, was compelled to wait two thousand years.

THE FINAL JUDGMENT.

Judgment, says Paul, comes first to the Jews, then to the Gentiles. For nearly two thousand years—*i.e.,* since Christ judged the Jews at the destruction of Jerusalem —the Gentiles have been under God's care, and the Gentile judgment must be near at hand.

The judgment of the Gentiles and the destruction of this physical universe will be simultaneous events.

Once God said, "Let the earth be created," and it was created. Some day, in His own good time, He will say, "Let the earth be destroyed," and it will be destroyed.

When will this earth end?

We answer, when the Gospel has been preached to all men.

The exploits of Livingston and Stanley show that the light of this century is beginning to shine even in benighted Africa, and the time must be near, with the electric flash encircling the globe, when it can be said that the Gospel *has* been preached to all men. Then, according to Christ, the end will come. This earth had a beginning, and it will have an ending. To individuals it ends at death. To you and to me, my friends, it matters little when it ends if we have Christ; without Him we must perish.

A Reply To Attacks On The Bible.
This was written in January, 1878.

THE Bible is the record of God's dealings with man. By it He spoke to the Jewish nation. By it Christ and the apostles thunder their proclamations across the ages since the destruction of Jerusalem, and on it we base our hope of eternal life.

In our defense of the Bible we shall review parts of it and attempt to show what it teaches.

"In the beginning," we read, "God created the heavens and the earth and all things that dwell therein, and pronounced it very good;" that He made man "in His own image," and gave him "a wife;" that he put the man and the woman into the Garden of Eden, and gave the man full dominion over all created things. And God commanded the man, saying, "Of every tree of the garden thou mayest freely eat; but of the tree of the knowledge of good and evil thou shalt not eat, for in the day thou eatest thereof thou shalt surely *die.*" We also read that Satan, in the form of a serpent, said unto the woman, "Ye can eat, and ye shall not die;" that thereupon the woman ate the forbidden fruit, and then induced the man to eat. That, soon thereafter, the "Lord God called unto Adam, and said, Where art thou? Hast thou eaten of the tree whereof I commanded thee, saying, thou shalt not eat?" The man said, "I did eat," and blamed it on the woman, and the woman blamed it on the serpent.

Now what happened?

And the Almighty was angry; He cursed the man, the woman, and the serpent; He pronounced a special curse upon each.

When Adam sinned, he threw himself into the arms of the devil. His posterity, in consequence of his surrender, came into being under a law of gravitation towards sin and death. We hold that a part of mankind are not only born under the power of "the wicked one," but are of his seed, and that their destination is perdition. We also hold that another part of mankind are of Christ's seed, and that their destination is heaven. "My sheep," says Christ, "hear my voice." The reason some people must be damned is because they have no ear to hear the Gospel of God's reconciliation with man, through the death and resurrection of Jesus Christ. By the death and resurrection of Christ, God became reconciled to human nature, and what the race lost by Adam's fall they gained by the ascension of Christ. Jesus Christ, by His death and resurrection, overcame the devil. He released man from his grasp, and thereby destroyed the cause of all sin, and thereby reconciled human nature to God. The effect of this action on them that believe is to release them from the power of sin; on them that believe not, to consign them with the devil to eternal damnation. No one will be damned without a chance to believe on Christ. If they reject Christ they must be damned. It is *their* fault; not God's.

"But," says a noted infidel (and this is his great point), "hell being such a terrible, awful place, and God being so *very* good, He won't send any one there." We answer,
God must sustain His government. Heaven is for the righteous. Hell for the wicked, Heaven would be a hell, if the wicked could get into it. Hell is for the devil's seed; heaven for Christ's seed.

This infidel denies the immortality of the soul.

"I am willing to give up heaven," he says, "to get rid of hell."

We prove the immortality of the soul thus: We read "that the Lord God formed man of the dust of the ground, and breathed into his nostrils the breath of life, and man became a living soul." (Gen. 2:7). Man, therefore, was composed of two substances, the dust of the ground and the breath of life, *i.e.,* matter and spirit.

We hold that "a spirit is a fluid. That it has many of the properties of caloric, electricity, galvanism, and magnetism. That it has also the power of assimilation, growth, and self-originating motion. That it has personality, feeling, intelligence, and will." When Adam was created, the Almighty breathed this vital fluid into Adam's body, and he then became a living soul. As soon as this vital fluid (or the Almighty's breath) entered into Adam's dust-formed body, it partook of the shape of that body; *i.e.,* it became congealed, and ever afterwards retained the form and shape of that body.

The prime element of the soul is this vital fluid which emanated from the Almighty, and it is *this* eternal spirit which makes the soul indestructible. "He that believeth on me," says Christ, "shall never die." Why? Because the life of the soul and body are *one.* The soul lives after it has left the body. Every human being is destined for heaven or perdition; because they have a soul, and *that* is immortal.

About a thousand years after Adam, we read that God saw that "the wickedness of man was great," and He repented "that He had made man," and said, "I will destroy man whom I have created from the face of the earth." There was only one righteous man in all the world. His name was Noah. "And God said unto Noah, the end of all flesh is come;" make thee an ark, for I am going "to destroy all flesh." And Noah *did as* the Lord commanded. Now what? After Noah and his family and his property were safely in the ark, "the fountains of the great deep were broken up, and the windows of heaven were opened," and the rain descended in torrents for forty days and forty nights, and every living thing on earth was destroyed—save Noah and his ark.

The point of this story is that God **kept** His word, and He always keeps His word.

What next? A thousand years after Noah came Abraham. "And God said to Abraham, get thee out of thy country, and from thy kindred, and from thy father's house, unto a laud that I shall show thee; and I will make of thee a great nation; and I will bless thee, and make thy name great; and thou shalt be a blessing; and I will bless them that bless thee, and curse him that curseth thee; and in thee shall all families of the earth be blessed." (Gen. 12:1-3). Now what? "And Abraham *did* as the Lord had spoken." Abraham's obedience was the foundation of God's favor. The Old Testament is the record of God's dealings with Abraham and his seed for two thousand years, *i.e.,* till the birth of Christ.

The New Testament, which is a record of Christ's life and principles, is simply a continuation of God's dealings with mankind. Christ endorsed the Old Testament in every possible way. He always spoke of it with the utmost respect, and said He came not to destroy "the law, but to fulfil it."

Infidels say the Old Testament is a horrible book, because it tells of the wickedness of the Jews; that it records murders, wars, rapine, and evils of all kinds. We answer, the Jewish nation contained bad people as well as good. "There were vessels of honor and dishonor" in that great nation. God's writers in the sacred volume put the bad in as a warning and reproof to the race.

But the New Testament concerns us more than the Old.

We analyze the New Testament thus:

In order to the full exhibition of Christianity it was necessary there should be: 1. A history of the life of Christ. This we have in the four gospels. 2. A sketch of what followed His resurrection. This we have in the Book of Acts. 3. A systematic exposition of the theory of redemption founded on the death and resurrection of Christ. This we have in the epistles of Paul. 4. A code of morality with injunctions and warnings against error. This we have in the whole New Testament. 5. An exhibition of the mature results of Christian faith. This we have in the first epistle of John. 6. A sketch of the futurity of Christ's kingdom. This we have in the book of Revelation.

The New Testament is just what we might suppose it would be, on the assumption that Jesus of Nazareth was what He pretended to be, viz. "God manifested in the flesh." The Bible, and especially the New Testament, is the visible link connecting God with man—this world with eternity.

Reasons Why Many Persons Are Going Down To Perdition

This was written in September, 1879. Perdition is the final abode of the lost, as Heaven is the final abode of the redeemed. The intermediate state is Hades. Hades is composed of two wards— one (for the righteous) called "Paradise," the other, "Hell." If one reaches Hell he is sure to reach Perdition. If one reaches Paradise he is sure to reach Heaven. Hades was emptied when Christ appeared, A.D. 70, and will be again at the final resurrection and judgment at the end of the world.

THE possibilities of human existence are appalling. Millions and millions of individuals have come and are coming into this world without any agency of their own. If most persons could have their choice I imagine they would keep out of it. And yet this is a magnificent world. It is full of beauty and blessings. On all sides happiness awaits us. God is wonderfully good. But man, in his fallen state, has brought vast evils upon the race, and we propose to show why many persons are going down to perdition. The possibility of such a condition is terrible; but I believe it is true, and I shall attempt to show that it is true.

Many persons are going down to perdition because they do not realize that there *is* such a place. We are told by a distinguished gentleman (he from Illinois) that there is no perdition. And we are told it with the sneer and power of a sharp-tongued orator; and many persons are in doubt whether there really is such a place. To the sneers of infidels, Christians appeal to the Bible. If the Bible is a lie, as some say, the Almighty is back of it, as they will find to their eternal sorrow some time.

Many men are going down to perdition because all men by nature are rebels against God. The whole world lieth in the Wicked One. Only those are saved who find the Savior. The rest are doomed to perdition. If the Bible is a lie, the Almighty is back of it. If Christ is an imposter, as some say, His awful power at the destruction of Jerusalem must satisfy the most skeptical that the Almighty is back of Him. For eighteen centuries Christendom has not known of Christ's appearing in judgment at the destruction of Jerusalem; but now that it has been revealed, it gives awful prestige to Christ's words. Every prediction He made concerning the destruction of Jerusalem, and the awful overthrow of the Jews was literally fulfilled. This fact gives an awful prestige to Christ's words; and it behooves skeptics to look before they resist the Almighty's only Son. The Jews resisted Him and their city was razed to the ground, and their national existence destroyed.

From the destruction of Jerusalem to Martin Luther, covering a period of fifteen long and weary centuries, the Almighty seems to have withdrawn all interest in human affairs. With Luther came light. With Calvin came light. With Wesley came light; and the race is getting light rapidly in this nineteenth century. We live in a fast age; in an age of steam, electricity, and printing. The scientific discoveries of this age are appalling. Edison and his co-workers descend upon us like a tornado.

Look at Grant. Twenty years ago he starved in Galena. The war came and he came. Today, September, 1879, he strides like a young god over the earth. Who shall gainsay this little man of destiny? The extraordinary attention paid him wonderfully indicates the prevailing unification of the race in these latter days.

God is wonderfully gracious. The good and bad alike share in His bounty. At all times the race is under His protecting care. Nothing is too small for His notice. He careth for the just and the unjust; but some time there will be a reckoning. The small and great, the dead and living, must stand before the Judge of all, and be sentenced to eternal life or eternal death. This thought is overpowering. The cares of this world, the lusts of the flesh, the deceitfulness of riches, and the pride of life, paralyze the mind; and we can hardly realize this stupendous fact. Is the soul immortal? Is there a heaven? Is there a hell? The Bible says the soul *is* immortal. The Bible says there *is* a heaven. The Bible says there *is* a hell; and *that* is all we know about it.

As we said at first, the possibilities of human existence are appalling. The fact of an eternal existence in happiness or misery is appalling. And we exclaim, why is it thus; and find no answer save in the Bible, and in the history of the race. If perdition is certain, heaven is also certain; and we can reach it by finding the Savior.

If God is omnipotent why does He not save all men? We answer, because they are not save-able. Some men belong to the devil's seed. There are two classes born into this world: Christ's seed and the devil's seed. Christ's seed go to heaven, and the devil's seed to perdition. They could not co-exist. Heaven would be perdition if the wicked could get into it.

We have some new ideas on the origin of evil. We hold that God is not responsible, as is generally supposed, for the evil existing in this world, but that the devil, His great personal antagonist, *is* responsible. We hold that all good comes from God, and all evil from the devil, and that these two great personal powers have been fighting for supremacy since the creation of the world. In the person of Jesus Christ, God and the devil fought it out, and God partly overcame the devil in that fight. Christ says, "whosoever believeth on Him that sent me *hath* everlasting life." The devil and his seed have no *disposition* to believe, and, therefore, must be damned. Man is a free agent. He can go to the right or to the left. He can choose good or evil. He can go to church or to a saloon, and end in heaven or perdition.

Such a man as Ingersoll says he can't believe in Christ; that he "can't see it," which is conclusive evidence that *he* belongs to the devil's seed, and must go down to eternal perdition. But it is not God's fault. Not even God can save the devil's seed. (See "The Two Seeds,").

Many people, at first, hear the Gospel with gladness, but are swept by the currents of infidelity, worldlines and sensuality into perdition.

The Gospel takes deep root in the hearts of some people, and they become the true followers of the Savior. They are the salt of the earth. They build churches, send missionaries to foreign countries, run Christian and benevolent associations, and make this world a decent place to live in. Destroy the influence of this class and it would be worse than Sodom.

German Rationalism, Unitarianism, Universalism, and all isms that bewitch one from the simplicity of the Gospel, as taught by Christ and Paul, are taking men down to perdition. In Luke, 16:19-31, we have an account of a man who got into hell. It is terrible reading, and it reads thus:

"There was a certain rich man, which was clothed in purple and fine linen and fared sumptuously every day. And there was a certain beggar named Lazarus, which was laid at his gate, full of sores, and desiring to be fed with the crumbs which fell from the rich man's table; moreover, the dogs came and licked his sores. And it came to pass that the beggar died, and was carried by the angels into Abraham's bosom. The rich man died also, and was buried. And in hell he lifted up his eyes, being in torments, and seeth Abraham afar off, and Lazarus in his bosom.

And he cried, and said, Father Abraham, have mercy on me, and send Lazarus, that he may dip the tip of his finger in water and cool my tongue, for I am tormented in this flame. But Abraham said, Son, remember that thou in thy lifetime receivedest thy good things, and likewise Lazarus evil things; but now he is comforted, and thou art tormented. And besides all this, between us and you there is a great gulf fixed, so that they which would pass from hence to you cannot; neither can they pass to us that would come from thence. Then he said, I pray thee, therefore, father, that thou wouldest send him to my father's house, for I have five brethren, that he may testify unto them, lest they also come into this place of torment. Abraham saith unto him, They have Moses and the prophets; let them hear them. And he said, Nay, Father Abraham; but if one went unto them from the dead they will repent. And he said unto him, If they hear not Moses and the prophets, neither will they be persuaded, though one rose from the dead."

Had this man believed in "Moses and the prophets" he might have escaped his horrible fate. Today men are going down to perdition because they have no saving faith in Jesus Christ. *Nothing short of personal union with Christ* will save a man from the hell recorded in Luke, 16:19-31. We believe, as a matter of fact, that many persons who expect to go up will go down. Compare the life and principles of the Savior with the life and doings of many professed Christians, to say nothing of the ungodly, and see how they fall short of Christian character.

Some persons who are going down to perdition: Whiskeymen, saloon-keepers, whoremongers, prostitutes, seducers of innocent virtue, willful liars, theatre-goers, horse-racers, (and their kind), tricksters in politics and business, and bad people of all grades are on the road to perdition.

This class are going down to an eternity of misery. This is a terrible, awful fact; and we would fain save all we can. All we can do is to point them to the Savior.

How do you know they are going down to hell? "By their fruits ye shall know them." "Whatsoever a man soweth that shall he also reap." They are sowing to the wind and they will reap a whirlwind. This class belong to the devil's seed, and perdition is their destination.

Writers and publishers of light literature are sending many to perdition. I imagine publishers do not realize their responsibility in sending out a book. No one can tell the effect of a book. It may save or damn a soul. Think of such a book as Paine's "Age of Reason," and all that class of books. Then think how immoral publications are flooding the land. The details of crime, as reported in most of the daily papers, are not fit for decent people to read; but thousands read them to their sorrow and ruin. There ought to be a law prohibiting such publications. They only debauch the public mind.

Our daily papers are greatly responsible for the interest many take in horse-races, foot-races, and other demoralizing shows. They might exert a strong influence against it if they were so inclined.

Extravagance is sending many to perdition. "The love of money," says Paul, "is the root of all evil;" and he is right. Most persons are on the grab for money. Day and night they think of money, money, money. They need money to keep up style, and they get it; but at a fearful risk. Some men would sell their soul for a ten-dollar bill. Think of the Savior—the greatest and purest being who ever lived on this globe. He was so poor He had not where to lay His head. If people thought less of style and more of their eternal destiny they would have a chance of reaching heaven. But money is all some people can see.

The theatres are sending many to perdition. "Do you think it harmful to go to the theatre?" Yes, decidedly. What would you think of the Savior's elbowing His way into a theatre to see a half-nude performance? The drama tends down, not up. Many a man has been ruined by frequenting theatres. If I had my way I would close every theatre in the land.

Weak men in the pulpit are sending some down.

I do not like to say anything against the pulpit, as it represents many pious and able men; but I must tell the truth without fear or favor.

HOW MODERN MINISTERS ARE MADE.

A pious parent, intending his boy for the ministry, sends

him to college, and then to a theological seminary. If able, a few years' foreign study and travel are added. Then he is "called." *i.e.,* he is put over a high-toned church on a large salary. He is expected to deliver two sermons a week and attend prayers. If a Presbyterian, he must preach Presbyterianism; if a Methodist, Methodism. Whatever the ism of his church he must preach it or "step down and out." Harassed and harnessed by the tenets of his church, no wonder that his sermons are stale. He whines through his discourse, says the prayer, and the people go home. Under this kind of preaching the churches often become cold and heartless.

Many people go to church because it is the proper thing to do. The ladies go to see each others' fine clothes, and the gentlemen to see the ladies. Holy Ghost preaching is unknown to many modern preachers. Many of them are after a large salary, with little work, and a gorgeous church equipage. No wonder there is no power in the church, and that many persons are going down to perdition.

We attended the preaching of an alleged divine in Boston about two years ago. Music Hall was packed, and the alleged preacher whined through a discourse about "Jesus." We were struck by his personal appearance. A massive gold chain conspicuously encircled his breast, and he seemed more interested in fast horses and "buck- boards" than in saving souls. We were not surprised to hear of his downfall.

Another distinguished divine, of thirty years' standing, recently shook two hemispheres by his alleged amorous exploits. Guilty or not guilty, he certainly was exceedingly indiscreet, and brought vast scandal upon the church. Our sensational friend Talmage recently made a brothel reputation which took him successfully through Europe. When alleged men of God like these scandalize religion, who can wonder that many immortal souls are going down to perdition?

Let our modern preachers look at Paul, the ablest and most successful preacher the world ever produced. He did not settle down on a high-toned church, and whine through a discourse twice a week, for a large salary. No, not he. He was after souls.

The people are ready to sustain a live preacher, and, if our pulpit friends would preach the Gospel, pure and simple, as Paul did, they would be sustained. They need not fear the Assembly or the Conference. See how Moody has shaken things up. No minister of modem times has been so well sustained, on both sides of the Atlantic, as Moody.

We knew Moody twelve years ago, when he was the laughing-stock of Chicago. His zeal was so great for the Master, that he used to go up to strangers, and say, "Do you love the Lord?" "Are you for Jesus?" Most people do not like to have their personality intruded upon in this way, and "Brother Moody" was considered by many people a nuisance. But these weaknesses are forgotten now. We see the work he has done, and thank God for Moody. Mr. Moody's knowledge of the Bible is wonderful; his delivery sparkling; his capacity to tell a touching story immense; and herein we see the outward cause of his success as an evangelist. But the real cause is that the Lord seems to have a work for him to do. "Every man to his work" is the law in Christ's kingdom, and Mr. Moody is doing his work in preparing the world for their judgment, which we believe is not far distant. If the Bible is true, our belief that we are rapidly approaching the Final Judgment is true.

As the Jews could not escape the "wrath of God," neither can the Gentiles. "We must all appear before the judgment-seat of Christ, and be rewarded according to the deeds done in the body." The reward of those who patiently continue in well-doing, "and seek for glory, and honor, and immortality," will be eternal life— an eternity of bliss. But to those who obey not the truth, but obey unrighteousness, indignation and wrath. "Tribulation and anguish," says Paul, "cometh upon every soul of man that doeth evil." But "glory, honor, and peace to every soul that worketh good." To the Jew first and also to the Gentile. The Jews, as a nation, had their judgment at the destruction of Jerusalem, and the Gentiles will have theirs at the end of the world.

Now that God is drawing near to earth we need the faith and simplicity and Holy Ghost power of Apostolic times.

These views ought to unite all who really *love* the Savior in Tabernacle form of worship, doing away with gorgeous and half-paid-for churches, to the end that the glory of God in these latter days may cover the earth as the waters cover the sea. Let us labor and pray for this grand consummation.

THE TWO SEEDS
This was written in June, 1881.

CHRIST'S parable of the sower, as recorded in Matthew, 13:37-39, shows that there are two classes of humanity born into this world, Christ's seed and the devil's seed; that one class are predestined for heaven, and the other for perdition; that the final destination of any individual depends on the source from whence he or she originated. If they came from Christ's seed, their destination is heaven. If from the devil's seed, their destination is perdition.

From this two-fold nature of mankind came John Calvin's idea of predestination. He got this idea, first, from Christ, and then from Paul; but he restated it with marked force, and it stirred the people of his day immensely.

It is not for us to judge whether an individual belongs to Christ's seed or the devil's seed. That will be revealed at the final judgment. But "by their fruits ye shall know them." If we see a person striving for honor, and glory, and immortality by patient continuation in well doing, we may rightfully judge that that soul loves the Savior, and is destined for heaven. On the other hand, if we see a soul carnally minded, and wholly given to worldliness and sensuality, we may rightfully judge that such an one belongs to the devil's seed, and is predestined for perdition. An individual may, apparently, belong to Christ's seed, and yet, in time of temptation, fall away. His falling is evidence he did not belong to Christ's seed. On the other hand, an individual may, apparently, belong to the devil's seed until he hears the Gospel; then, he becomes "converted," and commences a Christian life.

It may be very hard that some individuals should be predestined for perdition; but it is not God's fault. This condition of a part of mankind arises from the fact of the existence of the devil. We hold that the devil is an active personal being, almost co-equal with the Deity, and that he, like the Deity, existed from all eternity, and will continue to exist for all eternity. We hold that on no other ground is it possible to relieve the Deity from the responsibility of the stupendous evil existing in this world. We hold that God is not responsible for the evil existing in this world; and that He cannot prevent it. If He could prevent it, and did not, He would be unworthy of a God. He had the power to create this universe, but He has not the power to extinguish His uncreated personal antagonist, the Devil, who, Christ says, "was a murderer from the beginning," meaning thereby from the beginning of his uncreated existence. We entirely repudiate the idea that the Deity created the devil. God and the devil are both uncreated. They never had a beginning and they never will have an ending. This world was manifestly created as a battle-ground for God and the devil to test their respective power. In the person of Jesus Christ God and the devil tested their strength; and God so far overcame the devil in that death struggle as to give humanity eternal life, provided humanity would reach for it by faith in Jesus Christ. By this act of faith God and humanity unite in overcoming the devil. God holds out His hand, but humanity must seize it or continue in the grasp of the devil.

We hold that the Deity is infinitely pure, and wise, and good, and that He is almost omnipotent, but not quite; that He would be entirely omnipotent were it not for the almost equal cunning and power of His great uncreated antagonist, the devil, or the "Evil One," as the Revised New Testament has it.

THE PREDICTED FATE OF THE EARTH
Sunday Magazine.

THE Apostle Peter, in his second epistle, announced the approach of a time when "the heavens shall pass away with a great noise, and the elements shall melt with fervent heat; the earth also, and the works that are therein, shall be burnt up." What has modern science to say to the possibility of a catastrophe such as that shadowed forth in a comparatively unscientific age, eighteen centuries ago? Mr. R. A. Proctor, writing in his latest volume, "The Flowers of the Sky," remarks: "It is no longer a mere fancy that each star is a sun; science has made this an assured fact, which no astronomer thinks of doubting. We know that in certain general respects each star resembles our sun. Each is glowing like our sun with an intense heat. We know that in each star, processes resembling in violence those taking place in our own sun, must be continually in progress, and that such processes must be accompanied by a *noise and tumult,* compared with which all the forms of uproar known upon our earth are as absolute silence. The crash of the thunderbolt, the bellowing of the volcano, the awful groaning of the earthquake, the roar of the hurricane, the reverberating peals of loudest thunder, any of these, or all combined, are as nothing compared with the tumult raging over every square mile, every square yard of the surface of each one among the stars."

He proceeds to describe, with considerable circumstantiality, two appearances witnessed in the heavens within the last few years: In 1866, when a tenth-magnitude star, (that is, four magnitudes below the lowest limit of the naked-eye vision), in the constellation of the Northern Crown, suddenly shone as a second-magnitude star, afterwards rapidly diminishing in lustre; and in 1876, when a new star became visible in the constellation Cygnus, subsequently fading again so as to be only perceptible by means of a telescope. After noting the conclusions deduced from the application of the most improved instruments to these observations, Mr. Proctor, whose authority is second to none among astronomers, remarks: "A change in our own sun, such as affected the star in Cygnus, or that other star in the Northern Crown, would unquestionably destroy every living creature on the face of this earth; nor could any even escape which may exist on the other planets of the solar system. The star in the Northern Crown shone out with more than *eight hundred times* its former lustre; the star in Cygnus with from *five hundred* to many thousand times its former lustre, according as we take the highest possible estimate of its brightness before the catastrophe, or consider that it may have been very much brighter. Now, if our sun were to increase *tenfold* in brightness, all the higher forms of animal life, and nearly all vegetable life, would inevitably be destroyed on this earth. A few stubborn animalcules might survive, and possibly a few of the lowest forms of vegetation, but nought else. If the sun increased a *hundredfold* in lustre, his heat would doubtless sterilize the whole earth. The same would happen in other planets. Certain it is that if our sun ever undergoes the baptism of fire which has affected some few among his brother suns, one or other of these processes (if creation can be called a process) must come into operation, or else our earth and her companion worlds would forever after remain devoid of life."

PART II.
THE REMOVAL

SYNOPSIS
OF MY TRIAL
FOR REMOVING JAMES A. GARFIELD

WITH
LETTERS OF COMMENDATION
AND OTHER PAPERS.

PREFACE.

On February 4 I was sentenced to be hanged June 30, 1882, for removing James A. Garfield, and I herewith publish a synopsis of my trial. Scoville's fool theory and Spitzka's moral monstrosity lie, with the mean, diabolical spirit of the prosecution, convicted me. The only issue to be tried was: "Who fired that shot?" I, personally, or I, as the agent of the Deity. I say the Deity inspired the act and forced me to do it, and that He will take care of it. I say Garfield deserved to be shot. I say any President that will go back on the men who made him, and wreck the organization that elected him, and imperil the Republic, as Garfield did, deserves to be shot, and I was God's man to do it; Garfield gushers to the contrary. Posterity will say so, too, whatever this generation may say about it. I frequently get letters from school children; and they show a better understanding of the necessity for Garfield's removal than some old heads. The Lord takes no fancy stock in Garfield or any other man. I judge the world is divided into three classes on this Guiteau-Garfield business—fools, devils, and rational people. The fools and devils seem to predominate. Posterity will represent the rational people. There has been a deal of lying in this case. The latest is that if I am hung I want a crowd to see it. The fact is I want no one present save the officials, and they had better resign than kill God's man. I tremble for them and for this nation if a hair of my head is harmed.

Some people think hanging a horrible death. As a matter of fact, it is an easy death. I had rather be hanged than killed on a railroad, or go by fire or flood, or a painful illness. Mere physical death is nothing. If the Lord wants me to go to glory that way I am willing; but I am bound to make the best fight I can to vindicate my inspiration, and to that end I shall press my appeal to the court in banc by securing the best lawyers I can to represent me in banc. If all other remedies fail, I shall boldly appeal to the President for relief under my own hand.

Andrew Johnson pardoned Jefferson Davis. Davis sought to destroy this Nation. I sought to save it. Horace Greeley and Commodore Vanderbilt and other liberal and far-seeing men signed Davis' bail bond, and thereby brought upon themselves the wrath of certain disreputable newspapers and crank politicians. The Union League Club of New York assumed to criticize Mr. Greeley for signing Davis' bail bond, and thereupon Horace opened on the "blockheads" of said club in his usual vigorous style, which was somewhat like my own.

Should it become necessary for President Arthur to pardon me I presume he will follow his own wishes without reference to "blockheads," newspaper devils, or cranks, of high or low degree.

If the politicians and newspapers who were cursing Garfield last spring had any honor they would stand by me, especially the men who hold fat offices, which they obtained from my inspiration. Editors, not newspaper devils, may review this book. Newspaper devils are prohibited from reading it, as they are supposed to have no brains or disposition to appreciate it. I sell this book for two dollars, bound in paper. Purchasers can bind it to suit themselves. To the trade, eighteen dollars per dozen. Sold only by me. Mailed to any address on receipt of price. Photographs with autographs $9 per dozen or $1 each. (Send money by registered letter only).

I spit on adverse opinion on this subject. I say I am right. Garfield ought to have been removed, and I was God's man to do it. If I am murdered on the gallows this nation and the officials that do it will pay well for it. It will be a long time before the Almighty lets up on them. I had rather go to glory in June than to Auburn Prison for life as some people suggest. I want an unconditional pardon or nothing. I am a patriot, not a criminal, and that will be my character in history. This is the only view I press on President Arthur for a pardon, should it become necessary. In law this is insanity.

CHARLES GUITEAU.
United States Jail,
Washington, D.C. *March* 14, 1882.

MY CLOSING ARGUMENTS

President Garfield was shot July 2, 1881. He died September 19, 1881. I was indicted October 8, 1881. Trial began November 14, 1881. Verdict, Guilty. January 25, 1882. February 4, 1882, I was sentenced to be hanged June 30, 1882.

This case was fully reported in all the leading newspapers, and it is unnecessary to reproduce it here, except as it appears in the attached documents. I appeared as my own counsel in part, and on Monday, January 16, 1882, the following speech was published in the leading newspapers, and on the following Saturday I delivered it to the jury. I spoke two hours to a minute.

This is the newspaper report of it:

The demand for admission to the court-room was unprecedented in the long history of the trial. As early as 8 o'clock the crowd commenced to assemble in front of the court house, and when the doors were opened, at 9.30 o'clock, there was a desperate struggle for precedence. Inside of fifteen minutes the court-room was filled to overflowing, and Marshal Henry cried out: "Don't allow any person to enter the room." The crowd on the outside continued to swell in volume and soon degenerated into an angry mob. Deputy Marshals, court bailiffs and policemen vainly endeavored to quiet their mutterings, and it was not until near 11 o'clock that the excited mob dispersed, fully satisfied that the coveted admission was among the impossibles. The audience as to the sexes was about evenly divided; of the females in attendance fully two-thirds were of the strong-minded order. Quite a number of the women in attendance at the female suffrage convention occupied conspicuous seats. The District bar and the pulpit of Washington were largely represented. Congress was present in the persons of Representatives Harris, of Virginia; Van Voorhis, of New York; Herbert, of Alabama; Washburn, of Minnesota, and Klotz and Beltzhoover, of Pennsylvania.

The prisoner's counsel and his brother and sister were early arrivals. District Attorney Corkhill and Mr. Davidge were the Government's representatives. At 10.10 Judge Cox took his seat on the bench and the court was formally opened. The prisoner was at once brought in and escorted to the witness box. He was cleanly shaved and dressed for the occasion with especial nicety.

The Court. (To the Prisoner). You may proceed now.

The Prisoner: If the court please, gentlemen of the jury: The prosecution pretend I am a wicked man. Mr. Scoville and Mr. Reed say I am a lunatic. I certainly was a lunatic on July 2 when I fired on the President, and the American people generally think I was, and I presume you think I was. Can you imagine anything more insane than my going to that depot and shooting the President of the United States? You are here to say whether I was sane or insane at the *moment* I fired that shot. You have nothing to do with my condition before or since that shot was fired. You must say by your verdict sane or insane at the *moment* I fired that shot. If you have any doubt of my *sanity* at that moment you must give me the benefit of the doubt and acquit, *i.e.,* if you have any doubt whether I fired that shot on my own account, or as the agent of the Deity. If I fired it on my own

account I was sane. If I fired it supposing myself the agent of the Deity I was *insane*, and you must acquit. This is the law as given in the recent decision of the New York court of appeals. It revolutionizes the old rule, and is a grand step forward in the law of insanity. It is worthy of this age of railroads, electricity, and telephones, and it well comes from the progressive State of

New York. I have no hesitation in saying that it is a special Providence in my favor, and I ask this court and jury to so consider it. Some of the best people of America think me the greatest man of this age, and this feeling is growing. They believe in my inspiration, and that Providence and I have really saved the nation another war.

My speech, setting forth in detail my defense, was telegraphed Sunday to all the leading papers in America, and published Monday morning. And now I am permitted, by his honor, to deliver it to you. Only one mistake occurred in it, and that was my fault. I sent out a Christmas greeting, and the first paragraph of my speech was taken from a printed slip, and I omitted to erase the words, "Christmas, 1881," which appear a few lines from the top of the speech. The sentence improperly reads: "Today. Christmas, 1881, I suffer in bonds as a patriot." The words "Christmas, 1881," should have been erased.

And here I desire to express my indebtedness to the American press for the able and careful way they have reported this case. The American press is a vast engine. They generally bring their man down when they open on him. They opened on me with all their batteries last July, because they did not know my motive and inspiration when I shot the President. Now, that this trial has developed my motive and inspiration, their bitterness is gone. Some editors are double-headed. They curse you today and bless you tomorrow, as they imagine public opinion is for or against you, which shows a very low grade of character. I desire to thank my sister, brother, and counsel, for their services on this trial. I return thanks to the marshal and his aids, to the superintendent of police and his force, to the warden of the jail and his keepers, and to General Ayres and his troops for services rendered me during this trial. I return thanks to this honorable court, and to this jury, for their long and patient attention to this case.

I am not here as a wicked man, or as a lunatic. I am here as a patriot, and my speech is as follows. I read from the *New York Herald*. It covers over a page. It was sent by telegraph Sunday, and published in all the leading papers in America Monday:

81

GUITEAU'S SPEECH.

Production on which he relies for acquittal—Claim of inspiration for the good of the party—Enrolling himself as a patriot—Press criticism and expert testimony.

If the court please, gentlemen of the jury: I am a patriot. Today I suffer in bonds as a patriot. Washington was a patriot. Grant was a patriot. Washington led the armies of the Revolution through eight years of bloody war to victory and glory. Grant led the armies of the Union to victory and glory, and to-day, the nation is happy and prosperous. They raised the old war-cry, "Rally round the flag, boys," and thousands of the choicest sons of the Republic went forth to battle, to victory or death. Washington and Grant, by their valor and success in war, won the admiration of mankind. Today, I suffer in bonds as a patriot, because I had the inspiration and nerve to unite a great political party, to the end that the nation, might be saved another desolating war. I do not pretend war was immediate, but I do say emphatically that the bitterness in the Republican Party last spring was deepening and deepening hour by hour, and that within two or three years or less the nation would have been in a flame of civil war. In the presence of death all hearts were hushed, contention ceased. For weeks and weeks the heart and brain of the nation centered on the sick man in the White House. At last he went the way of all flesh, and the nation was in mourning.

Today, I am in the presence of this able and careful jurist and this jury, charged with wickedly and maliciously murdering the late President, and today, I suffer in bonds as a patriot.

There is not the first element of murder in this case. To constitute the crime of murder two elements must co-exist. First, an actual homicide; second, malice in law or malice in fact. The law presumes malice from the fact of the homicide. There is no homicide in this case, and therefore no malice in law. Malice in fact depends on the circumstances attending the homicide. Admitting that the late President died from the shot, which I deny as a matter of fact, still the circumstances attending the shooting liquidate the presumption of malice either in law or in fact. Had he been properly treated he probably would

82

have been alive today, whatever my inspiration or intention. The Deity allowed the doctors to finish my work gradually, because He wanted to prepare the people for the change and also confirm my original inspiration. I am well satisfied with the Deity's conduct of the case thus far, and I have no doubt that He will continue to father it to the end, and that the public will sooner or later see the special providence in the late President's removal. Nothing but the political situation last spring justified his removal. The break in the Republican Party then was widening week by week, and I foresaw a civil war. My inspiration was to remove the late President at once, and thereby close the breach before it got so wide that nothing but a civil war could close it. The last war cost the nation a million of men and a billion of money. The Lord wanted to prevent a repetition of this desolation, and inspired me to execute His will.

Why did He inspire me in preference to some one else? Because I had the brains and nerve, probably, to do the work. The Lord does not employ incompetent persons to serve Him. He uses the best material He can find. No doubt there were thousands of Republicans who felt as I did about the late President wrecking the Republican Party, and had they the conception, the nerve, the brains, and the opportunity and special authority from the Deity, they would have removed him. I, of all the world, was the only man who had authority from the Deity to do it. Without the Deity's pressure I never should have sought to remove the President. This pressure destroyed my free agency. The Deity compelled me to do the act, just as a highwayman compels a man to give him money, after placing a pistol at his victim's head. The victim may know it is absolutely wrong for him to give money that his wife and child need, but how can he keep it with a pistol at his head? His free agency is destroyed and he gives his money to save his life. This irresistible pressure to remove the President was on me for thirty days, and it never left me when awake. It haunted me day and night. At last an opportunity came, and I shot him in the Baltimore and Potomac depot. As soon as I fired the shot the inspiration was worked off and I felt immensely relieved. I would not do it again for a million of dollars. Only a miracle saved me from being shot or hung then, and there. It was the most in-sane, foolhardy act possible, and no one but a madman could have done it. But the pressure on me was so enormous that I would have done it if I had died the next moment. The Deity put it on to me, and I had to do it regardless of consequences to myself. In shooting the President I deny that I violated any law, human or divine. Nothing that the Deity directs a man to do can violate any law. I stand here as the agent of the Deity, and I shall call special attention to the specific acts of the Deity since July 2, wherein He has confirmed my original inspiration, to the end, that all intelligent people may see and believe that I simp-ly acted as His agent.

Had I shot the President on my own personal account no punishment would be too severe or too quick for me; but, act-ing as the agent of the Deity. I had no choice save to execute His will. There are more than thirty-eight cases in the Bible where the Deity has directed to kill for the good of the people, i.e., to save them from some far greater trouble.

Heretofore political grievances have been adjusted by war or the ballot. Had Jefferson Davis and a dozen or two of his co-traitors been shot dead in January, 1861, no doubt our late re-bellion never would have been, and this would have saved the nation a vast deal of trouble and expense, and nearly a million of lives. General Grant, after four years of bloody strife, sup-pressed one war, and Providence and I saved the nation one. As time advances the public will appreciate this fact more and more.

General Arthur, as President, is doing splendidly. No man can do better. I am especially pleased with his conciliatory spirit and wisdom toward the opposition. It is exactly what I wished him to do, viz. unite the factions of the Republican Par-ty, to the end, that the nation may be happy and prosperous.

The New York *Herald* of a recent date says:

If one compares the first two months of Garfield's Admin-istration, under the bad inspiration of Mr. Blaine, with the first two months of Mr. Arthur, he must say the comparison works entirely in Mr. Arthur's favor. The Garfield-Blaine policy was openly and distinctly proscriptive. It did not pretend other-

wise. It violated unblushingly every canon of civil service reform and every pretense of sound administration: it flung the
party into a furious turmoil, and, leaving aside entirely the remarkable and scandalous foreign policy which it made haste to
set on foot, it used the public offices without the least regard to
fitness or propriety to reward personal adherents of Mr.
Blaine, and to punish Republicans against whom there was no
charge of failure to perform their duties to the public.

"The country," says the *Herald*, "will give General Arthur
the heartiest support while it sees him reverse the policy of his
predecessor in many particulars, for both in home and in foreign affairs that policy, inspired by the demagogue whom poor
Garfield in an evil moment made his Secretary of State, was evil
and disgraceful, and only that."

In short, everybody politically is happy, save a few cranks,
and they will probably be happy soon. Happiness is catching.
The political situation today is just what I knew it would be last
June if Mr. Garfield was removed. Everything on this case so far
has gone about as I anticipated last June, which, is an evidence
of the Deity's confirmation of my act.

I have been in jail since July 2, and have borne my confinement patiently and quietly, knowing that my vindication would
come. Thrice I have been shot at and came near being shot
dead, but the Lord kept me harmless. Like the Hebrew children
in the fiery furnace, not a hair on my head has been singed, because the Lord, whom I served when I sought to remove the
President, has taken care of me.

My life has been rather a sad one. My mother died when I
was seven. My father was a good man and an able one, but a
fanatic on religion. Under his influence I got into the Oneida
Community at nineteen, and remained six years. Three years
after this, I was unfortunately married, and so continued four
years. My life in the Oneida Community was one of constant
suffering; my married life, the same; my theological life, one of
anxiety, but I was happier at that than anything else, because I
was serving the Lord. My life has been isolated. During my six
years in the Oneida Community I got estranged from my relatives. I might as well have been in a State prison or a lunatic

asylum. I never was able to forgive my father for running me into that community. If it had not been for this I should have had a far happier life. Forgetting the things behind I press forward. I have no doubt as to my spiritual destiny. I have always been a lover of the Lord, and whether I live one year or thirty I am His. As a matter of fact, I presume I shall live to be President. I have had this idea for twenty years, and it has never left me.

General Arthur is a good man every way. I happen to know him well. I was with him constantly in New York during the canvass. So with General Grant, Conkling, and the rest of those men. They have not taken an active part in my defense because it would not be proper. But I know how they feel on this case. They elected Garfield, and they know that under Blaine's influence he proved a traitor to them, and imperiled the Republic. Had Garfield shown the spirit and wisdom of Arthur he probably would have been alive today. But he sold himself body and soul to Blaine; and Blaine, is morally responsible for his death. Mr. Blaine is a good fellow personally, but he is a vindictive politician, and he wanted to get even with Grant and Conkling and Arthur for defeating him at the Chicago Convention, and Garfield weakly yielded himself to Blaine's influence, and it finally resulted in his death.

The prosecution have introduced certain witness who are guilty of rank perjury, and it has excited my wrath, and I have denounced them in plain language. I hate the mean, deceptive way of the prosecution. My opinion of the District attorney is well known. The defense has been unfortunate in having insufficient counsel, but notwithstanding this I expect justice will be done me, and my motive and inspiration vindicated.

People are saying, "Well, if the Lord did it, let it go."

The mob crucified the Savior of mankind, and Paul, His great apostle, went to an ignominious death. This happened many centuries ago. For eighteen centuries no men have exerted such a tremendous influence on the civilization of the race as the despised Galilean and His great apostle. They did their work and left the result with the Almighty Father. And so must all inspired men do their work regardless of consequences, and leave the result to the Almighty.

The worst that men can do is to kill you, but they cannot prevent your name and work from thundering down the ages. God always avenges those who injure His men. Christ's contemporaries crucified the Almighty's only Son, but He got even with the Jewish race at the destruction of Jerusalem, A.D. 70, when Titus, a Roman general, razed the city to the ground and slaughtered over eleven hundred thousand Jews, and from that day to this the Jews have been a despised and down-trodden race. The mills of the gods grind slow, but grind sure. Woe unto any man or men that persecutes God's man! The Almighty will follow them in this world and in the next. Take my own case. When the pressure to remove the President came on me, I spent two weeks in prayer to make sure of the Deity's will. At the end of two weeks my mind was fixed as to the political necessity of his removal, and I never have had the slightest doubt since about the divinity of the act or the necessity for it. Thus far the Deity has fathered the act to my entire satisfaction. He knows I simply executed His will and I know it, and a great many people are beginning to see it, and they will see it more and more as time advances. I put my life on the Deity's inspiration, and I have not come to grief yet, and I have no idea I shall: because, I do not think I am destined to be shot or hung. But that is a matter for the Deity to pass on, and not me. Whatever the mode of my exit from this world, I have no doubt but that my name and work will roll thundering down the ages; but woe unto the men that kill me privately or judicially! The Deity and one man are always a majority, and will prevail against all the men ever born. Abraham and the Deity were a majority. Noah and the Deity were a majority. Jesus of Nazareth and the Deity were a majority.

Over eighteen hundred years ago the Savior of mankind was born in poverty and obscurity. He moved up and down Judea and spoke as one having authority. Vast multitudes followed him He cast out devils, healed the sick, restored the blind and diseased, told the multitude who He was and what He came for—that God, the Father, had sent Him to point to the race the way to eternal life. This wonderful being had nowhere to lay His head. He had no money. He had no friends. He never travelled. He never wrote a book. He was hated, despised, and finally crucified as a vile impostor. Then, back He went to the bosom of the Father. During His ministry He drew around Himself a few despised individuals who were as poor as Himself. They had no money and no standing in society, and were mostly fishermen. Outwardly, like most other great events in human history, Christianity at first was an absolute failure. It was like a seed planted and it had to grow little by little. Time has developed it into a gigantic tree, covering nearly the habitable globe.

God's men are generally poor. Martin Luther, the great reformer of the sixteenth century, was a pauper all his life, but he served God with amazing effect, and his name went into the history of his time as the foremost religious man of his age. Luther revolutionized the religious thought of fifteen centuries, and today his name is revered by Protestant churches. But Luther had a hard time getting in his work. He was persecuted and imprisoned, but out of it all the Lord delivered him.

Today I am a poor man, because I left a good law business in Chicago in 1877 to try and do my duty in enlightening mankind on theology. I went into theology to serve the Lord and preach the gospel. I had as much trouble to get in my work on theology as Paul did. He hungered and thirsted and was naked and had no certain dwelling-place, and preached the gospel as he understood it. Since he left this world his work and name have come down the ages. Christ and Paul did their work and left the result with the Almighty Father, and I do the same. Christmas, 1878, I was in Saint Louis. I was in very reduced circumstances. I had been on theology a year. I had spent the year travelling, mostly in the East, trying to preach the gospel by lecturing and selling my lectures in Washington, New York, Boston, Chicago, and other cities. I felt the Lord put this work on me, and I did the best I could. I had no friends and little money. Christmas, 1877, I spent in Philadelphia. I was well fed and clothed, and was trying to lecture. Christmas, 1876, I was in Chicago and was working with Mr. Moody and writing my lecture on Christ's second coming, A.D. 70, wherein I show that

His second coming occurred at that time in the spiritual world, and that Christendom for eighteen centuries has lost its reckoning concerning this great event! My mission was to enlighten mankind in reference to the second coming of Christ—a subject that has caused the wisest theologians in the Christian Church for eighteen centuries a vast deal of thought and has probably ruined thousands of immortal souls! I spent three years in this business and received nothing but poverty and contempt for my services and trouble. But I expect the Deity will take care of me hereafter on that. This is the reason I am today a poor man. Had I stuck to my law business either in New York or Chicago, I should have been a rich man to day, but I had other work to do. My book, The Truth, contains my theology. It cost me trouble enough, and I have no doubt but it is official. During the three years I was on theology I incurred some small debts which I have not yet been able to pay. A thousand dollars would pay every dollar I owe. Some men owe a hundred thousand dollars and are considered high-toned. The prosecution have made a great noise about my owing some board bills, but that has no bearing on this issue whatever; whether I owe five cents or twenty thousand dollars. As a matter of fact, I owe about a thousand dollars. But that has nothing to do with this case in any manner, shape, or form. I understand Mr. Corkhill, who has taken it upon himself to dig up my circumstances, owes a hundred times more than I do. I always pay when I have the money, but there was no money in theology, and I knew it when I went into it. I did the best I could considering my circumstances, and that was all the Lord wanted of me. As Paul says, "I fought a good fight, I finished my course, I kept the faith," and I am sure of my reward.

In August, 1879. I left Chicago and spent several months in Boston, trying to push the sale of my book, but it was new and few persons appreciated it. I left Boston in June, 1880, and went to New York to take an active part in politics. I was a "Grant man," but I was pleased with Garfield's nomination. I wrote a speech entitled "Garfield against Hancock," wherein I sought to show that the Republic would be imperiled by Hancock's election. I gave this speech to the leading Stalwarts and they were pleased with it. It had a certain ring and they noticed it. I made their personal acquaintance at the Fifth Avenue Hotel and at the headquarters of the Republican National Committee, and was always well received by them. I judge they thought me a bright man and a good fellow. I was in New York from June, 1880, to March, 1881, when I came to Washington. I was an applicant for the Paris consulship, and pressed my application in March and April. Owing to General Garfield's unwise use of patronage he began soon after his inauguration to wreck the Republican Party, and continued so to do till the day he was shot.

Garfield was a good man, but a weak politician. His nomination was an accident. His election was the result of the greatest activity on the part of the Stalwarts, and his removal a special providence. As soon as he was inaugurated he foolishly made Mr. Blaine—the worst enemy that Grant and Conkling had—his Secretary of State and bosom friend. Blaine used Garfield to crush Grant and Conkling and Arthur—the very men that made Garfield President. Without the extraordinary efforts of Grant, Conkling, and Arthur and the rest of the Stalwarts, Garfield never would have been elected. Every man of sense will admit this, whatever his politics. Soon after Robertson's appointment the Republican Party began to heat up. This was about the middle of May. By the 1st of June it was red hot. By the 1st of July it was white hot. If this spirit had not been killed by the President's removal, the nation would soon have been in a flame of civil war. Our late rebellion cost the nation nearly a million of men and a billion of money, and it desolated the hearth-stones of the Republic. To prevent a repetition of this desolation the removal of the late President was necessary. By his removal the Republican Party was cemented and the nation today is happy and prosperous. And today, I suffer in bonds, because, I had the inspiration and nerve to remove the President that the nation might live!

I now review the case since July 2, and call special attention to acts of the Deity wherein He has taken special pains to protect me and confirm my inspiration, to the end, that all men may see, and seeing, may believe in my inspiration.

The political situation attracted my attention about the 20th of May—*i.e.,* at the time Messrs. Conkling and Platt, the then Senators from New York, resigned. The public mind was greatly excited over their resignation, and it greatly perplexed me, and I grieved over it, because I was at the National Republican headquarters in New York during the canvass, and I knew that Grant and Conkling and Arthur had elected Garfield.

When I saw that Garfield, under Blaine's vindictive spirit, was proving a traitor to the men that made him it grieved me to the heart, and I prayed over it. "If Garfield was out of the way," thought I one night in my bed, "everything would go well." Things seemed to be going from bad to worse under his leadership, and I foresaw another desolating war as the result of it. For two weeks I prayed over the possibility of the President's removal. The more I prayed about it and the more I looked at the political situation the more I saw the necessity for his removal. Finally, after two weeks of earnest prayer, I decided that the Deity had called me to do it, and I commenced preparation for it. This was about the 1st of June. From that day to this. I never have had the slightest doubt as to the divinity of the act or the necessity for it. An opportunity came, and I shot him on July 2. Not being a marksman he lingered till September 19, when he passed quietly and gently away, the Lord thereby confirming my inspiration.

There was a special providence in his dying in New Jersey. I undertake to say the Deity allowed him to die there to protect me from the possibility of legal liability for simply executing His will. Should this jury condemn me to be hung, the Deity has probably fixed the law so that their verdict cannot be legally enforced. It is the opinion of some of the ablest members of this bar that this court has no jurisdiction to try this case.

I now call attention to other acts of the Deity confirming my inspirations.

I went to the Baltimore and Potomac depot on the 2nd of July, and shot the President twice. Only one ball took effect. I would not do it again for $1,000,000. It was the most insane, foolhardy act possible. No one but a madman could have done it. But I would have done it any time after June 1 if I had known

I was to be shot dead the next moment. I had no power to prevent it. My free agency was entirely destroyed. I was under duress. In law, any one under duress is not responsible for his act. How do we know you were under duress? My word for it. No one else can know this fact but the Deity and I. I know it and the Deity knows it, and He has taken special pains thus far to protect me. I might have been shot dead at the depot, and probably would have been had not the Deity protected me. I had to do my duty to the Deity and to the American people, regardless of consequences to myself. Do the act and let the Deity take care of it is what I did do, and He has taken care of it thus far to my entire satisfaction.

I would have been hung or shot a hundred times last summer if I had not been in jail—one of the finest in America—and protected by the national troops. The Lord uses men to serve Him and protect me. The bitterness against me was caused by the public not knowing me or my motive. My trial has informed them, and today, I can walk all over Washington or New York safely. No one wants to shoot or hang me now, save a few cranks, who are so ignorant they can hardly read or write. High toned people are saying, Well, if the Lord did it, let it go."

The President did not die before his time. If the Lord bad not wanted him he would not have departed. Physical death is nothing. All men have died; all men will die. The President might have been taken off by a railroad accident, or slipped on an orange peel and broken his neck. During the war thousands of brave boys on both sides went down without a tear. Their mangled remains lie buried in many a grave. They left their homes and loved ones and suffered as I do today for their country.

Just think of it! If it be true absolutely that Providence and I saved the nation, why should I not be a hero, and the equal of Washington and Lincoln and Grant? Many people are beginning to see that I have saved the nation. Listen to this from a Philadelphia gentleman. I judge him to be a high-toned lawyer from his style and penmanship. I withhold his name:

Philadelphia, *January* 1st, 1882.

Dear Sir: I wish you a very happy New Year. You have cemented the Republican Party and saved the nation. Your name will live in history and go down through the ages linked with the patriot Brutus. The results that have followed your act are the best evidences of your inspiration.

Julius Caesar, the greatest Roman of his age, was assassinated by Brutus in the Roman forum, wherein congregated the wealth, the wit, and the beauty of the Roman empire. An elocutionist has sent me a new version of Shakespeare's "Brutus on the death of Caesar," which I here give in part. This is the new version of it:

Friends, countrymen, and lovers!

Hear me for my cause, and be silent that you may hear.

Believe me for mine honor, and have respect to mine honor that you may believe. Censure me in your wisdom, and awake your senses that you may the better judge.

If there be in this assembly any dear friend of Garfield, to him I say Guiteau's love to Garfield was not less than his. If, then, that friend demand why Guiteau removed Garfield, this is Guiteau's answer: Not that Guiteau loved Garfield less, but he loved his country more. Had you rather that Garfield were living and die in war than that Garfield were dead to live in peace? As Garfield loved Guiteau, Guiteau weeps for him; as he was fortunate, Guiteau rejoices at it; as he was a good man, Guiteau honors him; but by the Deity's inspiration Guiteau removed Garfield for the good of his country.

The prosecution have introduced certain disreputable witnesses—to wit, one Reynolds; to wit, one Shaw; to wit, one English, and others like them. These witnesses are hardly worth my notice. Reynolds, a sneaking Government detective, came to my cell about July 20 and appeared exceedingly cordial and pretended to be my personal friend. I had not spoken to him for years, although I read law in his office in 1868. His testimony in general was correct; but I hate the mean, deceptive way he and Corkhill got it. Shaw, I officed with in New York in 1872 and 1873, and have known nothing about him since. He pretends I told him I was going to emulate the example of Booth and kill some great man. This is absurd on its face. Is is likely I would wait ten years to remove General Garfield when

Grant and Conkling and scores of far more prominent men than Garfield, were living during the ten years since Shaw pretends I told him I would emulate the example of Booth? The fact is I never mentioned Booth's name to Shaw in any possible way. Shaw's pretense is a wicked and malicious falsehood, without the slightest foundation in fact. This man Shaw was indicted for perjury in New Jersey and came near being convicted. The court told him from the bench, so I am informed, that he ought to be in State prison for perjury. At all events, he told a willful lie about me. English was in jail under $10,000 bail for libeling Mr. Winston, of the New York Mutual Life Insurance Company, and I got him out after several weeks of strenuous effort, for which he paid me my fee and subsequently sued for the money. It was a gross piece of impertinence on his part, and his attorney subsequently told me he commenced the suit under a misapprehension.

I now review briefly some of the evidence to show that I tell the truth when I say that the Deity inspired me to remove the President; that He forced me to do it, and that He has taken care of it.

The President was shot on July 2, and I went immediately to police headquarters and remained fifteen minutes, and then to the jail. I was taken to the jail in a carriage by Detective McElfresh and Lieutenant Austin and two officers. We drove rapidly so as to avoid the mob. As soon as we were under way McElfresh said, "We were not any too soon. They were organizing," meaning, that if I had remained at police headquarters I would have been hung or shot immediately. McElfresh said, Why did you shoot Garfield?" I said, "Because he was wrecking the Republican Party, and that there would have been another war in this country soon." He said, "There are a great many people of your way of thinking." "Of course there are," said I.

This shows why I shot the President, and kills the Paris consulship idea. I would not have taken any office from the President after June 1, under any circumstances; not even a Cabinet appointment.

Mr. Brooks, Chief of the Secret Service interviewed me in my cell July 2 about 12 o'clock—that is to say, the first night I was in jail. This interview is thus reported in his testimony:

James G. Brooks. Chief of the Secret Service Division of the Treasury Department, was then called to the stand by Mr. Scoville, and in reply to questions made the following statement:

I had an interview with the prisoner at midnight on the 2nd of July. When I entered the cell I announced my name and position. Mr. Guiteau was in bed. He rose up and exhibited great anger and excitement, and wanted to know why I came at that time of night and disturbed his rest and quiet, and he told me to go away. I retorted pretty hotly that it ill-became a murderer to complain about his rest and quiet when he had disturbed the rest and quiet of the nation, and plunged it into grief. He came at me and said he was no murderer. He was a Christian and a gentleman. I said that I, too, professed to be a Christian, and thought that if he had ever taken God into his counsel in this matter he would not have done so wicked a thing.

He said that he had taken God in account; that he had thought over it, and prayed over it for six weeks, and the more he thought and prayed the more satisfied he was that he had to do this thing. I endeavored to argue with him, but he would have no argument. He had made up his mind that he had done it as a matter of duty, and could not listen to any argument about it. His mind was made up, and he did not want to be disturbed. He spoke, also, of his being a Stalwart, and asked me whether I was a Democrat. I said no; I was a Republican. "And a Stalwart?" "Yes: and a Stalwart."

"Then," said he, "you can appreciate my motives in doing this thing. You can see it is a political necessity. What I did I did from patriotic motives to unify the party." We talked probably half an hour. I kept crowding him, and he talked eloquently. I told him I came to learn who his accomplices were. He said he had no accomplices; no soul on earth knew of what he was going to do but himself. I intimated that we were about to make two or three arrests. He said, "Don't do it. If you do, you will arrest innocent men. There was no man connected with me in this thing." I questioned him about the purchase of the pistol. He told me where he purchased it. The next day I visited him. He was calm then, and quite glad to see me. He gave me the details of his work—how he commenced; how he watched the President; how he was going to shoot him two weeks before when he was deterred by seeing the poor, sick wife on the arm of her husband. He told me, also, that he was lying in wait for him one night near the White House when the President came out, and his first impulse was to remove him then. Somehow he was restrained from doing so. He followed the President to Mr. Blaine's house, and waited for them to come out. He could see Mr. Blaine arguing, and striking his hands, and talking very earnestly. The President, in his turn, would be striking his hands and talking, and he made up his mind that they were conspiring against the liberties of the people, and that the President must die.

I suggested to him then: "If your hand was stayed when you saw the wife of the President on his arm; if your hand was stayed when the President was alone, going to Mr. Blaine's house, how came it that you did not recognize that as an intimation from God that He did not want you to destroy this man?"

I forgot his reply, but it was an evasive one.

The Prisoner. It was that I only had authority to remove the President, not Mrs. Garfield.

The Prisoner. It is proper to say that Mr. Brooks has stated the conversations which occurred, between us very correctly indeed. He said that everybody was against me. I said I don't care if God Almighty is for me. I will take my chance, and after a while the people will be with me, and today they are with me.

Mr. Scoville. Did you report your interviews to any one?

The Witness. To Mr. Corkhill and Attorney-General MacVeagh.

The Prisoner. Mr. MacVeagh is a Christian man, and that is the reason he did not want to have anything to do with this case. That is the reason the New Jersey authorities did not want to have anything to do with it. They didn't want to get the Lord down on them. That is the place to try this case. You cannot try it here.

Mr. Scoville. Did he say anything in regard to that being the first rest he had had for six weeks?

96

The Witness. He did. He said that he had an excellent night's sleep—the first good night's sleep he had in six weeks.

The Prisoner. I felt light-hearted and merry as soon as I got into the cell. I felt happy because I had been true to God and the American people, and everything from that day to this has gone about as I expected. Everybody is happy except a few cranks, and I don't care about them. Mr. Garfield did not die before the Lord wanted him. If the Lord had not wanted him he would not have gone. He let him go to Elberon to remove him gently and gracefully.

This interview with Mr. Brooks I consider a special Providence in my favor. I talked with him freely about the Deity, my inspiration, and the political situation, which showed the condition of my mind on July 2, when I was precipitated on to the President. By no other man could I have proved the condition of my mind at the time I fired on the President. His testimony, I have no doubt, settled this case in my favor in the minds of many people. Mr. Corkhill and his stenographer, whom I took for a *Herald* reporter, interviewed me on July 3, and I told them, in a two-hour's talk, all about the Deity, my inspiration, and the political situation, for which the President was responsible. I also repeated this talk on July 4 in the presence of Corkhill, Bailey, the stenographer, and Mr. Scoville. I also told them emphatically I did not think the President would recover, because I did not think the Deity wanted him to recover, which proved to be correct, as he died on September 19. Mr. Corkhill wickedly and maliciously had Bailey's note-book destroyed so I could not prove by it what I said on July 3rd and 4th on my inspiration.

Mr. Brooks interviewed me, expecting to discover a conspiracy. I told him that my inspiration alone did it and that no one was associated with me. He listened carefully to my story, and he believed it, and dropped his conspiracy idea.

A vast deal of rubbish has got into this case on both sides. The issue here is, who fired that shot, the Deity or me? Had I fired it on my own personal account no punishment would have been too quick or too severe for me, and this is why I protected myself by going to jail and having the national troops

97

ordered out. I knew I would be shot or hung at once if I was not protected by the jail and the troops. I knew the President's removal would cause the greatest excitement, and my only safety was to get beyond the reach of the mob until the populace knew my motive and my inspiration. I am greatly indebted to General Sherman, General Ayres, and General Crocker, the warden of the jail, for protection. Had it not been for their vigilance, especially General Crocker's, I should not be here. General Crocker has been a solid friend to me from the start. The President's lingering illness and the suppression of all my papers, wherein I talked of the Deity's precipitating me on to the President, made a bitter feeling against me. This trial has developed my motive and my inspiration, and today the people consider me a patriot and a great man.

The prosecution have made a great flourish with their insane experts. The only insanity in this case is what these experts call transitory mania—*i.e.*, the Abraham style of insanity. There are thirty-eight cases of Abrahamic insanity in the Bible—*i.e.*, of illegal killing, resulting from the possession of transitory mania by divine authority. It was on this ground—to wit, transitory mania, that Sickles, McFarland. Cole, Hiscock, and other supposed criminals were acquitted. In the case of Cole the jury found him sane immediately before and after the firing, but they were uncertain as to his mental condition at the moment of firing, and they asked the court what their verdict should be. The court said they must give the defendant the benefit of the doubt, and they did so, and he was acquitted.

If a single man on this jury has the slightest doubt as to whether I fired that shot on my personal account, or as the agent of the Deity, he is bound under the law to give me the benefit of the doubt and acquit me. The prosecution have attempted to show by their paid experts that I was not suffering from transitory mania at the time I fired on the President. But what do they know about it? Absolutely nothing. Had I plenty of money I could get fifty reputable experts to swear I was insane, absolutely, at that time. I take no stock in the shape of the head or the hang of the tongue, or in the opinion of experts on either side of this issue.

I read the following from an able newspaper article, entitled "The Guiteau Experts." It is pointed and well written, and I give it entire. It comes from the Athens of America, Boston:

"The Guiteau Experts.—The Government experts in Guiteau's case seem to be having things very much their own way, and will probably succeed in getting him hanged, provided they succeed in getting the jury to accept their opinions as to his sanity or insanity. But will they do this? Are we to hang a man simply because a certain number of superintendents of lunatic asylums believe him sane? Are we to hang a man on mere opinion, the truth or reason of which cannot be judged of by common men? Do the lives of men in this country legally depend on the mere judgments of any twenty, fifty, or one hundred men who claim to know more than other men as to what diseases, delusions, or impulses that strange thing, the human mind is liable to, but who cannot so communicate the grounds of their opinions as to enable other men to judge of their truth or error? These men never saw, handled, or examined a human mind. They can only observe its manifestations through the body, and can only guess, like other people, at the causes of its mysterious and erratic operations. Are men to be hanged on the strength of their guesses? There are, we suppose, in this country three, or perhaps five hundred men—physicians, so called—who make a specialty of treating diseases of the human body where there is but one who makes a specialty of treating diseases of the human mind. But though diseases of the human body are so much more extensively studied and treated, and so much easier to be ascertained and judged of than are diseases of the mind, we have very little confidence of the knowledge of those many physicians as to the nature or causes of our bodily diseases. But even this is not all. These experts not only give their opinions that Guiteau is sane now, but also that he was sane on the 2nd of July, five or six months ago. Even if he is sane now, what do they know or what are their opinions worth as to whether he was, or was not, sane six months ago? They apparently have no reason for thinking that he was sane in July, except that they think he is sane in January. Would it not be just as sensible for them to say that, because he has no fever or delirium tremens on him today, therefore he could have had none on him six months ago? This kind of reasoning implies that they hold that if a man was insane in July he would undoubtedly have continued to be insane until January; or, what is substantially the same thing, that if a man is once insane he will always remain so. Now, this, we think, is very likely to be the rule in the asylums under their own control; that they seldom or never cure anybody that comes under their care, and we ought to be thankful for this information, for it enables us to know where not to send our insane friends if we wish to have them cured. In this theory of theirs, that once insane always insane, the cases in which they report the patient as ' discharged cured must be presumed to be cases in which the victims never were insane, but were simply sent to them on 'the certificate of two physicians,' who knew just as much about insanity as it was necessary for them to know, or as they cared to know, in order to earn two or three dollars for certifying their opinions.

"If these experts have really any reliable knowledge beyond that of other men as to the operations of minds diseased or not diseased, why do they not give us some reasonable explanation of the conduct of Guiteau in killing a man in open day and before a multitude of people, and making no attempt to escape, and all this when he had no personal malice toward his victim, and no rational prospect of gaining anything by his death? Are such acts as this common to human experience—so common as to imply disorder in the mind of the actor? Do all the experiences of all the bedlams on earth explain such a phenomena as this consistently with the sanity of the agent?

"When these experts are confronted with this question they are confounded. Instead of telling us how a sane man could do such an act they stammer out 'wickedness,' 'depravity,' 'evil passions.' But what 'evil passion?' Was it the evil passion of avarice or jealousy or revenge, or any other particular 'evil passion' that is known to induce men to commit murder? No; it was evidently none of these. But it was (as these experts would have us believe) simple 'wickedness,' 'depravity,' 'evil passions.' They can give no answer more definite than that. Such answers as these might perhaps pass in some schools of theology which hold that a virus of simple 'wickedness,' 'depravity,' or 'evil passions' was incorporated into the very nature of our first parents and by them transmitted to all their posterity. But when they are offered in a court of justice, where a man's life is at stake, they are not merely shameful, they are infamous. Men are not to be hanged in this country upon any theory that theologians or others may hold as to an ancient transaction between Adam, Eve, and the devil.

"Those experts have had thousands of insane persons under their care. Many of these persons have committed homicides or other violent assaults. All of them, or nearly all of them, were supposed to be liable to commit acts dangerous to themselves or others. The insanity of no two of them showed itself in the same way. But they were all saying and doing things daily that were just as absurd and irrational as was the act of Guiteau. And because their acts, whether violent or not, were so absurd and irrational, these experts have no doubt that the actors were insane. But when Guiteau does an absurd and irrational act they hold that he is not insane, but simply 'wicked,' 'depraved,' under the control of his 'evil passions.' And yet they can give no reasons—that are capable of being comprehended and judged of by common minds—why Guiteau's absurd and irrational act is not as good proof of his insanity as the absurd and irrational acts of others are of theirs.

"Even the witches were not hanged on such absurd testimony as this."

Spiritology and not craniology is the science that will sooner or later solve all questions of insanity. The possession of a spirit compelling one to do or not to do is the only way to solve the question of insanity. Let these paid experts study spiritology as taught by the Savior, and they will get more truth than they can out of craniology.

I am in receipt of a large mail, representing the progressive thought of the nation, which I now call attention to, as it shows the public feeling toward me. I withhold the names. I have probably a thousand letters awaiting my inspection in my office in the jail, which I shall examine as soon as possible.

I give a few, showing the tone of the American people. I annex letters from the East and the West and the North and the South and taking in all classes of society.

I recently received a telegram from Boston, as follows:

All Boston sympathizes with you. You ought to be President.

LETTERS FROM SUPPORTERS

A HOST OF ADMIRERS.

A Chicago lawyer sends this:

Chicago, *Dec.* 30, 1881.

> **Hon. Charles Guiteau:** I have watched your trial from the beginning with great interest, and am firmly convinced of the truth and justice of your defense. Be of good cheer. Your acquittal is assured, and you will come forth from this trial honored and respected. The American people delight in so striking an evidence of pluck and sagacity, and will surely sustain you.

Memphis. Tenn.

Hon. Charles Guiteau:

> **Very Dear Sir:** Allow a fellow attorney to wish you a happy New Year, and pray that your trial may soon come to an end, and that you may be honorably acquitted, as you deserve a better home than the one provided by the authorities at Washington. We think you are justified in that you were inspired to do the deed for which you are being tried.

South Pueblo, Col.

Jan. 1, 1882.

> Ten thousand citizens of the Centennial State hail you as a martyr to the cause of human freedom.

This is from Wisconsin:

What a pity that a Republican form of government allows you to suffer for an act you surely intended for its benefit. May God bless you and hasten the time when you will be set free. Your name is sung all over the land as a national hero.

New Haven, Conn.

December 31, 1881.
Hon. Charles Guiteau:

Dear Sir: Please allow a high-toned American citizen to thank you for demonstrating to fifty millions of people

in the glorious United States, and all Europe, Asia, and Africa, with the islands of the sea added, that you believe in liberty of conscience, freedom of thought, and are not afraid to express it. Sir, your example in the past few weeks will go thundering down the ages, and do more to extinguish gag-law than was ever done before.

Maintain your high-toned dignity and you are O.K. This is but a feeble expression of a large majority of the educated and cultured people of the United States.

Yours in the cause of free speech and liberty.

The Prisoner Continues: My little speeches have done more to break this prosecution than half a dozen of the best lawyers in America could do. I have always spoken for right, for justice, for vindication. I have had no intention to make this trial a farce. The prosecution have vilified me outrageously. I had to defend myself or be crushed like a craven.

Concordia, Kan.

January 1, 1882.
Hon. Charles Guiteau:

Dear Sir: I have been a close observer of the proceedings in your trial from the newspaper reports, and will assure you that your defense is daily gaining public favor in Kansas, and it is the opinion of the best men of the country here that your inspiration saved the Republican Party, and the time is not distant when you will be soundly acquitted and your fame flash across the country, and your inspiration will enlighten both the eastern and western hemisphere, and you may be assured of the heartfelt sympathy of every genuine Republican in Kansas, in this, your hour of affliction, who will ever attribute to you the honor and credit of saving, by your inspiration, our grand old Republican Party.

Philadelphia,

New Year's Day, 1882.

We wish to your honor a happy new year,
We hope that the hour of your freedom is near,
For your stainless acquittal we'll heartily pray,
As we read your career in the court-house each day.

All Philadelphia speaks in your praise,
To be chief of our nation your honor they'd raise.
That they will not see you by Corkhill to fall
Is the earnest resolve of our citizens all.

Davidge and Porter shall not get their way,
These bloodthirsty scoundrels have too much to say,
But they cannot be blamed, for their wages are high,
And we all know what evidence dollars can buy—

But little care you for themselves or their jaw,
For you greatly outshine them in smartness and law.
Your conduct this month back we all have admired,
And we feel fully certain you had been inspired

To make that removal by one daring deed,
For which we shall never allow you to bleed.

Protestant, Catholic, Quaker, and Jew,
We send our best wishes to Charles Guiteau.

We bid you be firm, determined, and brave,
And from Corkhill's vile meshes our hero we'll save.

New York,

January, 1882.

Hon. C. Guiteau: You do not place J.K. Porter's pay high enough. He gets $25,000 instead of $5,000, and those experts, (doctors), get from $1,000 to $3,000 instead of $5,000. They are wasting money that does not belong to them. Their testimony amounts to nothing. Keep things hot for them.

This man says Mr. Porter is a high-toned lawyer. Porter may lose some of his tone on this case. Mr. Porter was employed by General Arthur last October, before he knew the facts of this case.

Attorney-General MacVeagh examined my papers and sent Mr. Brooks to interview me, supposing there was a conspiracy, on July 2 and 3. I satisfied Mr. Brooks there was no conspiracy, and that the Deity had inspired me to remove the President, and he so reported to the Attorney-General, who then decided to have nothing whatever to do with this case.

Had President Arthur been as well advised as to the facts in October as he is today Mr. Porter would not be in this case. So with Davidge. Corkhill is booked for removal, and has been since General Arthur became President.

This man thinks I am better than Jeff. Davis:

Washington,

Jan. **3, 1882.**

In your speech to the court you may well argue that

105

if the leaders of the late rebellion, and especially Jeff. Davis, who is responsible for thousands of noble lives and millions of treasure sunk in war—Jeff. Davis, the arch criminal of the country—is allowed to go without punishment, you, who have but removed one man, and a politician at that, should certainly be treated with indulgence and clemency.

That is good logic.

It has been said that when the Deity and I removed the President a blow was struck at Republicanism. But I say the Republic was endangered by the President, and hence the necessity for his removal. I say that I saved the nation and the Deity confirmed the act, and the American people are satisfied with it. The American people are the most magnanimous people on the globe. All they want is to understand a matter and then they can give a righteous judgment. They admire brains and pluck, and go for it every time.

On June 16, two weeks before the President was shot, I used these words in an address to the American people.

> "Ingratitude is the basest of crimes. That the President, under the manipulation of his Secretary of State, has been guilty of the basest ingratitude toward the Stalwarts, admits of no denial. The expressed purpose of the President has been to crush General Grant and Senator Conkling, and thereby prepare the way for his renomination in 1884. In the President's madness he has wrecked the once grand old Republican Party, and for this he dies."

When I wrote these words I had been in a mania for thirty days; I had groaned under the political situation. I was in a reverie or trance. In the same address I used these words (I cannot render my feelings as Booth or Jefferson could, but I will do it in my humble way. I am supposed, for the moment, to recover from the mania. I think what the public will say when they find the President is shot, and I reel and stagger under the thought, I am about to remove the President. But God's will, and not mine, be done)—

"I had no ill-will toward the President. This is not murder. It is a political necessity. It will make my friend Arthur President, and save the Republic.

(A feeling of the war comes over me).

"Grant, during the war, sacrificed thousands of lives to save the Republic. I have sacrificed only one."

"I shot the President as I would a rebel if I saw him pulling down the American flag." [And here is the inspiration on the 16th of June.] "I leave my justification to God and the American people; and today, six months after the shot was fired, the Deity has repeatedly confirmed the act, as indicated by my experience as set forth in this speech, and the American people are satisfied to let this prosecution go by default."

On June 20, in the same address, I used these words, "The President's nomination was an act of God. The President's election was an act of God. The President's removal is an act of God."

A GENUINE CHRISTIAN ON THE GUITEAU CASE

I now call attention to a remarkable letter, entitled "A Genuine Christian on the Guiteau case." It is a public letter addressed to Mr. Scoville, and came to me providentially:

"Why torture your head about witnesses? Rivet your trust in Jehovah. Has He not already twice snatched your client, Guiteau, from the jaws of death? Be assured then, He will not desert you or him. I am told, sir, you are a 'Christian '—Guiteau we know is. Then throw to the winds insanity as a defense. Go boldly to trial demanding the recognition of God's supremacy. That it was His will Garfield should die is already proven. Had the bullet missed would it not have been providential? As it hit, was it not equally providential? Who but an infidel would say God had not the power to stop the leaden messenger? All Christians agree if God willed it otherwise it would have been otherwise. Could He not have

107

palsied Guiteau's arm had He wished? When Guiteau raised his weapon in His name would He not have stopped him, as He did Abraham of old, had it been His will? Isaac was rescued by God. Garfield was killed by God. Fifty millions of people went down upon their knees imploring his life. God answered them with death. Their prayer was, 'Oh spare our President, if it be Thy will.'"

Rev. Mr. Morgan (in Church of Heavenly Rest)—

"God had refused to prolong the life of our beloved President. He had refused it deliberately, and because it was best to refuse it."

Let Christians be sure of that. Let them know that God is always right. Let them kneel before the body of the dead President and say: "Our Father which art in Heaven, the blow is heavy. Thy providence is dark, but Thou knowest best—we can trust Thee when we cannot understand Thee."

Rev. Henry Ward Beecher (in prayer)—

"Thou Lord, hast laid Thy hand heavily upon this nation. Thy servant Thou has taken to Thyself in a way that fills us with shame and horror. We believe that Thou art anointing this great people and by this great sorrow raising us to a higher plane."

Rev. Mr. Crawford (Forty-second Street Methodist Episcopal Church)—

"Garfield's loss was a great one to the nation, but the wisdom of God could not be questioned, as He did all things for the best."

Rev. Dr. Morgan Dix (Trinity)—

"God made the world; He governs it. His never-failing providence ordered all things in heaven and earth. Whatever cometh hath a meaning. The events of the hour and the day are not the result of chance. God it is who orders or permits whatever occurs on earth, in heaven, in hell, above, below, around us. It may be there are those who do not feel in all this (the assassination) that God is chastening, afflicting, punishing, visiting."

Dr. Talmage—

"Garfield's death accomplished more than his life in setting forth the truth that when our time comes to go the most energetic and skillful opposition cannot hinder the event."

The Doctor (in prayer)—

"God bless this dispensation (the shooting of Garfield) to the nation, and may the people yet shout, ' Hallelujah, the Lord God Omnipotent reigns!'"

Rev. Dr. Storrs (Brooklyn)—

"Today I ask you to hear the voice of God in the lessons which He brings to us through this sad and strange and unexpected dispensation of His providence. Men sometimes say the cause of providence is not in it at all; it was mere human mortals; it was the insanity of the mind disordered. But God's providence controls the wills of men."

Rev. Dr. Bellows—

"Already blessings manifold had followed the shooting of the President, and the effect of that good influence was seen throughout the whole nation. Sublime confidence in God was reached when we could say from the heart, 'Though He slay me, yet will I trust in Him.'

God did not permit His ways to be placed under our microscopic inspection."

Clearly, Guiteau, was inspired from on high. Let this nation dare harm a hair of his head and it may go out in blood. God issued this order once, (and He may a second time:) "Put every man his sword by his side, and go in and out from gate to gate, throughout the camp, and slay every man his brother, and every man his companion, and every man his neighbor. There fell of the people that day about three thousand men."

If God's wrath is again stirred He may slay, not three thousand, but fifty millions—*i.e.*, the entire American people."

GUITEAU CONTINUES

This is a strong statement, but it is not too strong. Beware, ye nations of the earth, who incur the wrath of the Almighty!

The French nation incurred the wrath of the Deity and it came to grief. The bloody French revolution devastated that nation like a tornado of fire and blood. The old Roman Empire, the greatest government on earth for centuries, incurred the wrath of the Deity, and it too was swept out of existence. The Jewish nation, God's favored nation for two thousand years, incurred the wrath of the Deity when they crucified the despised Galilean, and it too went down in war and desolation.

Beware, ye Americans, that you do not incur the wrath of the Deity by dealing unwisely by me, for I tell you the truth and lie not, when I say I am here as God's man. He inspired the President's removal and has taken care of it, and I expect He will vindicate me, even if this nation rolls in blood! Put my body in the ground if you will; that is all you *can* do. But thereafter comes a day of reckoning. The mills of the gods grind slow, but they grind sure, and they will grind to atoms every man that injures me.

Beware, ye Americans! Beware!

American slaveholders put John Brown's body in the ground, but they paid for it during the war in blood and desolation.

> John Brown's body lies mouldering in the ground,
> But his soul went marching on.
> Glory hallelujah! Glory hallelujah!
> John Brown's soul went marching on.
> Glory hallelujah! Glory hallelujah!

"Vengeance is mine," saith the Lord; "I will repay." The Almighty always indicates His man. Beware, ye Americans, how you treat me, lest His wrath be kindled and you go down in blood and desolation.

Life is an enigma. This in a strange world. Often men are governed by passion and not by reason. The mob crucified the Savior of mankind, and Paul, his great Apostle, went to an ignominious death. This happened many centuries ago. For eighteen centuries no men have exerted such a tremendous influence on the civilization of the race as the despised Galilean and His great apostle. They did well their work and left the result with the Almighty Father, and so must all inspired men.

I count myself fortunate, indeed, that my case has been tried before so able and careful a jurist. I am glad your honor is a gentlemen of broad views, Christian sentiment, and clear head. I appear before your honor in a dual capacity: First, as a prisoner indicted for "murder;" secondly, as my own counsel in part, as I have a right to do under the law of every State in the Union. Certain witnesses have excited my wrath by their perjury, and I have denounced them in plain language. For this I have the example of the meek and lowly Jesus. How does this sound!

"Ye generation of vipers!" "Ye scribes, Pharisees, hypocrites, how can ye escape the damnation of hell?" Christ denounced iniquity in plain language and so do I.

In general, I am satisfied with your honor's proposed instructions, but I would humbly suggest that the jury be charged as follows: That if they believe that I believed it was right for me to remove the President, because I had special divine authority for so doing, they will acquit, on the ground that I was overpowered by the Deity, *i.e.,* that I was suffering from transitory mania. Sickles, McFarland, and Hiscock were acquitted on the ground of transitory mania.

Your honor's instructions cover this ground in part, but not quite so strong as I here state it, and I now ask your honor to charge as suggested.

I ask it in the name of the American judiciary, of which your honor is so distinguished a member. I ask it in the name of the American people, whose representative in this case your honor is. I ask it in the name of the Deity, whose servant I was when I shot the President. I ask it for the sake of your honor's judicial reputation and for the sake of the Deity's inspiration and my vindication. Your honor has suggested that the law of jurisdiction in this case may be different from what some of the leading Washington lawyers say it is. Should it be necessary to have your honor pass finally on this issue, I expect we shall find plenty of authority to show that your honor has no jurisdiction. I am also of the opinion that the court in banc will so decide if necessary. The judiciary of this District is not surpassed by that of the ablest judiciary in this Union. Chief-Justice Carter is the peer of any justice on the American bench and so are his associates.

And now, gentlemen, I must close.

Two months ago you left your homes and loved ones to listen to this case. I have no doubt but you have given it your most solemn and prayerful attention, and that your verdict will be "not guilty." as charged in the indictment.

To hang a man in my mental condition on July 2. when I fired on the President, would be a lasting disgrace to the American people, and I am sure you so understand it. The American people do not want me hung. They are saying. "Well, if the Deity did it, let it go." The mothers and daughters of the Republic are praying that you will vindicate my inspiration, and their prayers I expect will prevail. A woman's instinct is keener than man's, and I pray you listen to the prayers of these ladies. How would your mother and wife and daughter vote on this case? Have you any doubt but they would vote for an acquittal? And why should you not do likewise? There is not the first element of murder in this case. You might as well hang a man for murder during the war as to hang me. Under the law, as given by his honor, you can acquit me with entire credit to yourselves.

Physical death has no terrors for me. Suppose it possible that I should be sentenced to be hanged in thirty days. I may die in twenty-four hours. I shall not go until my time. I have always been a praying man, and I think I stand well with the Deity. I am sure I do in this case, for I certainly never should have sought to remove the President had the Deity not pressed me into it.

It is said that if I know the "difference between right and wrong" in removing the President, I violated human law, and ought to be hanged. But this is not the law, and, I say, the President's removal was right, because I had divine authority to do it. Admitting for the moment that I did violate the law of this District against murder, I reply, what of it? Thousands of persons have violated the letter of the law with impunity. If I violated the law, I did it under divine pressure, for the good of the American people, and they are willing to let this case go by default. In our Western domain thousands of Mormons are daily and nightly violating the law, but the United States Government do nothing to vindicate the dignity of the law. During the last decade Mormonism has spread with frightful rapidity, and today nothing but another war can suppress it.

The Federal Government is responsible for Mormonism. Let the President and Congress suppress this gigantic, spiritual, and social despotism. If I were President I would clean out these detestable Mormons in some way, and that right speedily.

And now, gentlemen, I leave this case with you.

At the last great day you and all men will stand in the presence of the Deity crying for mercy and justice. As you act here so will be your final abode in the great hereafter. I beg you do not get the Deity down on you by meddling with this case. I beg, for your own sakes and for the sake of the American people, and for the sake of generations yet unborn, that you let this case alone. You cannot afford to touch it. Let your verdict be that it was the Deity's act, not mine. When the President was shot his Cabinet telegraphed to foreign nations that it was the act of a "madman," and it will be far better every way that it be officially decided that it was the act of a "madman."

The newspaper report of my delivery continues as follows:

Guiteau then proceeded to read from a newspaper his extended "address to the jury," given to the press on Sunday last. His manner to the casual observer seemed as completely self-possessed as usual, but, behind the outward appearance of composure, there was an intensity of feeling which was only held in control through the undoubted strength of will and nerve which the prisoner has shown all the way through. His excitement was betrayed by a slight hectic spot upon each cheek of his usually colorless face, and by the unusual deliberation with which he began and for some time continued to speak. Whether this excitement was from the merely superficial effect upon his emotions, naturally incident to the occasion, or whether it proceeded from a deeper and more overpowering influence, it were difficult to divine. Whatever the origin or character of the feeling, it finally gained the ascendency over his powers of control, and, as he reached that point in his speech, "I have always served the Lord, and whether I live or die"—he broke down completely, stopped, tried to choke down the rising lump in his throat, but found it impossible to keep back a genuine sob. Taking out his handkerchief he buried his face in it for a few seconds, wiped his eyes, and with a determined effort started on again. After this incident the prisoner continued to read his address, occasionally adding brief comments upon the text. All appearance of nervousness gradually wore off. and with the utmost composure the prisoner read on with an attempt at every conceivable form of oratorical, rhetorical, and dramatic effect. His description of the taking off of the President was given with striking effect. At times he closed his eyes or turned them heavenward, waving his body back and forth, sinking his voice to a whisper or raising it to a high treble. At times the intensity of his utterances seemed to react upon him, but the effect was only transitory, and with the exception of one instance noted there was no other indication of his breaking down. At frequent intervals he paused to emphasize some sentence or sentiment by repeating it or commenting upon it. At one time, pausing, he leaned toward the jury, and emphasizing with his head and hands, said with great solemnity of utterance: "I tell you. gentlemen, just as sure as there is a God in heaven, if a hair of my head is harmed, this nation will go down in blood. You can put my body in the grave, but there will be a day of reckoning."

PUBLISHED ADDRESSES AND REPORTS

AN ADDRESS TO THE AMERICAN PEOPLE

On January 26, the day after the verdict, I wrote and published this address:

To the American People:

Twelve men say I wickedly murdered James A. Garfield. They did it on the false notion that I am a disappointed office-seeker. My speech they say made no impression on them. I am not surprised at their verdict, considering their class. They do not pretend to be Christian men, and therefore did not appreciate the idea of inspiration They are men of the world and of moderate intelligence, and therefore are not capable of appreciating the character of my defense. According to one of them, "We all had a grog at each meal and a cigar afterwards," which shows their style and habits. Men of this kind cannot represent the great Christian nation of America. Had they been high-toned Christian gentlemen their verdict would have been "Not guilty, because of insanity." The mere outward act of shooting would have been the same, whatever the motive. If I had been a disappointed office-seeker, which is absolutely false (as I prove by my papers and by Mr. Brooks' testimony on July 2 and 3) the outward act of shooting would have been the same, as if I had been directed by the Deity to do it, or believed myself so directed to do it, (which is the literal truth), as I prove by all my papers and talk on the subject. This jury had not sufficient intelligence to see that point, and entirely ignored the political and patriotic necessity for the act, which all Christian and intelligent people see. For this reason I am entitled to a new trial if for no other, and we have a prodigious amount of exceptions. I want to employ two or three first-class lawyers to take charge of my case. The principal point will be to show the non-jurisdiction of this court to try this indictment, because the President died in New Jersey. The authorities on this point are conflicting, but some of the best lawyers in America say, that the predominance of authorities are against the jurisdiction of this court. I desire the court in banc to pass upon this question, and have no doubt but the high- toned, Christian gentlemen representing the Washington court in banc, will give it their most careful attention, to the end, that if the Deity *intended* to protect me from legal liability herein, by allowing the President to depart gracefully and peacefully in New Jersey, that I have the benefit of the Deity's intention. I consider it a special providence in my favor, and I ask the court in banc so to consider it. I have received some checks, but many of them have proved worthless, which shows the low character of the men that send them. I need money to employ counsel. There are many people in America that believe in God and in my inspiration, and that

I am a patriot. To you, men and women of America, I appeal. I ask you in the name of justice to come speedily to my relief. Come in person or by letter. If you send money, send a postal order. With competent legal help I can get out of this, with the Lord's help, and I am sure of that. But good lawyers do not work for nothing. I want to employ two or three first-class lawyers to represent me in banc. If I had had competent counsel I should not have talked so much in court, but I disagree with the theory of Mr. Scoville, and it has made it unpleasant for both parties and has been a great damage to my defense. Judge Porter says I am right; and I agree with him, although I know he has abused and vilified me outrageously, when I had no alternative save to answer back, which I did in my usual plain way. T have been convicted, but the verdict cannot be enforced until June in any event, and probably not until September. I give myself no anxiety on account of the verdict. I hardly expected an acquittal; the most I expected was a disagreement, and then I proposed to test the question of jurisdiction in the court in banc. It is purely a legal question, and if the opinion of some of the best lawyers at the American

119

bar is sustained by the banc, it will end this case. I can get a hearing on this in April. I make a special appeal to the ladies of America to come to my rescue. Some of them have written me delightful letters, and I ask each and every one of them to respond to the extent of their means, and to see me in person if possible. I return my sincere thanks for their letters and sympathy. You ladies believe in God and in my inspiration, and that I have really saved the nation a great trouble and a great expense, to wit; another war. Last spring General Garfield had the Republican Party in a frightful condition, and it was getting worse every hour. Today, everybody of sense is satisfied with General Arthur's administration, and the country is happy and prosperous. Only good has come from General Garfield's removal, which is conclusive evidence that the inspiration came from the Deity. He has repeatedly confirmed my acts since July 2. Therefore, let all persons quietly acquiesce in the expressed will of the Deity. I am God's man in this matter, just as truly as the "despised Galilean" was God's man. They said He was a blasphemer and a glutton, &c. &c. and it seemed a small thing for His acquaintances to kill Him; but His death stirred the wrath of the Almighty, and He got even with them forty years later, at the destruction of Jerusalem, A.D. 70, and He will get even with the American people if a hair of my head is harmed. God will vindicate me even if this nation rolls in blood! Mere physical death is nothing to me. Under the law I cannot be executed in any event until June. I may die a dozen times before then, so I have no trouble about that. I shall not go before my time. I had rather be hung, so far as physical death is concerned, than die from a painful illness or meet with a railroad or steamboat accident. I hardly think I am destined to be hung, and therefore give myself no thought on that: but I am anxious to have my character and inspiration vindicated. To that end I need help, as herein mentioned. My friends need not be ashamed of me. Some people think I am the greatest man of this age, and that my name will go into history as a patriot by the side of Washington and Grant.

CHARLES GUITEAU.
United States Jail, Washington, D.C.

AN ADDRESS REGARDING MAIL AND AUTOGRAPHS

On February 2, I wrote and published this address:

A tramp says I stole his shirt. All statements of this kind are false. I never had anything to do with tramps or disreputable characters. I am high-toned; too high-toned for newspaper devils to notice, and I want them to let me alone. I never saw such a diabolical spirit as some newspapers have towards me; especially those that were cursing Garfield last spring. Since he was shot they have deified him and cursed me for doing the very thing they said ought to be done—viz. remove him! When God formed a man that had the brains and nerve to do it, these newspaper devils deify Garfield and curse God's man! But the Deity will get even with these fellows. If I were dead these devils would not be satisfied. If I had been President and wrecked the Republican Party, as Garfield did, I say I ought to have been shot, and posterity will say so, whatever this perverse and crooked generation may say. "Ye generation of vipers, how can ye escape the damnation of hell?" It is hard to tell how some newspaper men will escape that place if they continue to slander God's man.

My mail comes to the jail now. Any friends wishing to see me in person or write to me can do so. Any one having sent me an important letter and received no answer can write again, and I will see that it is answered. No notice given to anonymous or crank letters.

Photograph with autograph, $1, or $9 per dozen. (Autographs 25 cents). This photograph is a great improvement every way on the sitting of July 2 taken by Bell. My hair is parted and my beard off, and I look ten years younger. It is an historical picture, and any one can get it by sending me the price, and in no other way.

Under no circumstances will I allow my relatives or any one else to have anything to do with my body. If necessary I shall will it to some large cemetery. I shall probably need it myself for some time yet. Scoville's proposition is simply infamous and barbarous and not to be tolerated for a moment.

CHARLES GUITEAU.

United States Jail, Washington, D.C.

REPORT OF MY SENTENCING

On February 4 I was sentenced to be hanged on June 30, 1882. The leading papers published the following report, prepared by the New York Associated Press:

Mr. Scoville, counsel for the prisoner, then filed a motion in arrest of judgment, which was overruled by the court, and exception taken.

The Prisoner. I desire to ask, your honor, in my own behalf, if there is anything I need to do before your honor to preserve my rights in banc. I expect to have two or three of the best lawyers in America, but I want to know whether I must make any motion in order to preserve the record for them.

The Court. Every right shall be preserved.

The Prisoner. How much time have I in which to present my exceptions?

Mr Scoville then stated that he understood under section 845 of the Revised Statutes that he had until the next term to file his bill of exceptions.

The Court. No, not exactly that; there is no particular time fixed for preparing the exceptions. The term will be kept open.

Mr. Scoville. How long will I have?

The Court. The term will be kept open as long as you desire.

The Prisoner. I do not desire any advantage shall be

taken of me. I expect to have my lawyers procured shortly, and they will pull me through the court in banc.

Mr. Scoville. I have till the 1st of March to file my bill of exceptions?

The Court. Yes.

The Prisoner. That **is** understood.

The District Attorney. Let it be understood, then, that the bill of exceptions shall be in by the 1st of March.

Mr. Scoville. If I can do it in a week I will.

The Prisoner. I am here and I do not propose to leave this matter to you. I have my opinion of you as a lawyer. You convicted me with your jackass theories and consummate nonsense.

Mr. Scoville. I move to postpone the final execution of judgment in this case to a reasonable time beyond the next term of court, not exceeding thirty days after the end of said term.

The Prisoner. Do I understand that it is necessary to pass sentence until the matter is passed upon by the court in banc?

The Court. Yes; sentence is passed, but the execution is deferred.

The Prisoner. Within what time will your honor pass sentence?

Mr. Scoville. Keep quiet.

The Prisoner. You keep your mouth still. I am doing this matter myself. You convicted me by your wild theory and consummate asinine character all through. If the case had been kept entirely away from you I would have had two of the best lawyers in America, and there would have been no conviction. I had letters from them, and could have had them last October. I care nothing about your intentions. I want brains and experience. Let me alone and I will pull out of this. You got me into this trouble.

The District Attorney. The duty is now imposed upon me to ask the court to pass sentence in accordance with the verdict.

The Prisoner. I ask your honor to defer that as long as you can.

The Court, (to the prisoner). Stand up. (The prisoner rose). Have you anything to say why sentence should not be pronounced?

In a quiet voice the prisoner began his speech, but after he had delivered himself of two or three sentences his manner became more agitated. When he came to his prediction that the American nation would roll in blood he raised his voice to its highest pitch, and brought his clenched hand down with nervous force to emphasize his declaration. When he referred to the death of Christ he gave his voice that declamatory roll which throughout the trial has characterized his allusions to religious matters.

His response to Judge Cox's question was as follows: Guiteau's Speech.

I am not guilty of the charge set forth in the indictment. It was God's act, not mine, and God will take care of it. He will take care of it, and don't let the American people forget it. He will take care of it and every officer of this Government, from the Executive down to that marshal, taking in every man on the jury, and every member of this bench will pay for it, and the American nation will roll in blood if my body goes into the ground and I am hung. The Jews put the despised Galilean into the grave. For a time they triumphed, but at the destruction of Jerusalem, forty years afterward, the Almighty got even with them. I am not afraid of death. I am here as God's man. Kill me tomorrow if you want to. I am God's man, and have been from the start.

Judge Cox then proceeded to pass sentence, and after some preliminary remarks said:

You will have due opportunity of having any errors I may have committed during the course of the trial passed upon by the court in banc, but meanwhile it is necessary for me to pronounce the sentence of the law—that you be taken hence to the common jail of the

District, from whence you came, and there be kept in confinement, and on Friday, the 30th day of June, 1882, you be taken to the place prepared for the execution, within the walls of said jail, and there, between the hours of twelve and two P.M., you be hanged by the neck until you are dead, and may the Lord have mercy on your soul.

During the reading Guiteau stood apparently unmoved, his hand resting on the table and with his gaze riveted upon the judge. It was the longest time he had stood up in court. When the final words were spoken he struck the table violently and shouted:

And may the Lord have mercy on your soul. I'd rather stand where I do than where that jury does and where your honor does. I'm not afraid to die. I stand here as God's man, and God Almighty will curse every man who has had a part in procuring this unrighteous verdict. Nothing but good has come from Garfield's removal, and that will be the verdict of posterity on my inspiration. I don't care a snap for the verdict of this corrupt generation. I would rather a thousand times be in my position than that of those who have hounded me to death. I shall have a glorious flight to glory, but that miserable scoundrel, Corkhill, will have a permanent job down below, where the devil is preparing for him.

After apparently talking himself out the prisoner turned to his brother, and without the slightest trace of excitement conversed for some minutes before being taken from the court room.

Letters to My Attorney

These letters were published February 20 and addressed to my attorney, Hon. Charles H. Reed:

Mr. Reed: I will give you and Mr. ____and Gen. _____ my note, payable one year hence, for $5,000 each if you will get me out of here. I think you can do it on the ground of the non-jurisdiction of the court I have just written to my brother to make this offer to Gen. ____ . I depend on him to secure General ____ and I depend on you to secure Mr. ____ . Please call with Mr. ____ without delay. I presume I could make $50,000 next winter lecturing if I get out of this. I have an offer of $500 per night for six nights from Boston now.

Yours truly,
CHARLES GUITEAU.

United States Jail,
Washington, D.C. *Feb.* 11, 1882.

Mr. **Reed:** I consider the non-jurisdiction of the court my strong point. I asked Judge Cox before I was sentenced if I ought to do anything or make any motion to preserve my rights in banc, and he said "no." Now, I wish you would see him and Mr. ____ immediately and find out positively if it is necessary for me to make a formal motion before Judge Cox to press this point in banc. If so, I desire it made at once. I presume Judge Cox will allow it on the ground that he misled me.

Yours, &c.

CHARLES GUITEAU.
February 14, 1882.

AN INTERVIEW WITH MY BROTHER

A Brooklyn newspaper recently published a lengthy interview with my brother. John W. Guiteau, of Boston, and I extract from it. The interview is headed "**Guiteau,**" and is about me:

Has he much hope of escape from the sentence of the court?

He says he eats well, sleeps well, and feels well, and it is of no consequence to him what becomes of his body. He says they may bury it, but they can't harm him; he is God's man. And he always says, with great excitement of manner, pounding the table, that if he is harmed this nation will roll in blood; "but," he adds, "as a matter of fact, I expect to live to be President; but if my time has come, I am as well satisfied to be hanged, if God

126

wills it, as to die any other way." He says "future generations will yet see, and the American people will yet see, that I am a patriot and have saved the nation from war under the inspiration of Deity." He seems to have great hopes upon the motion for a new trial, and the exceptions to the jurisdiction of the court, and believes that it was a special providence, in order to save his life, that the President was permitted to be removed to New Jersey and die there. He also thinks that public sentiment among the best people is rapidly changing in his favor; not that they believe in his insanity, but in the truth of his inspiration, which is his only defense for the act. He said to me: "I notice that you keep saying in the papers that I am insane; that always makes me mad; I am no more insane than you are, and never have been. You and Scoville are both cranked on this defense. You both need some of my brains." He says he had transitory mania on the 2nd of July and for a month previous; and that is his true and only legal defense, and would have been successful, as in the case of Cole and Sickles, if the case bad been bandied by an able lawyer like General Butler. No one not familiar with the traits be has inherited from his family can appreciate the tenacity with which be depends upon the exact truth as a defense, and it was because be considered that the facts were violated by the witnesses and the attorneys on both sides that be became so denunciatory in court. He wanted the record right, as be repeatedly said in court, and has since said to me, in order that future generations may be enabled to judge truthfully of his character and act.

MY MARRIED LIFE

Annie J. Dunmire.

This lady has taken upon herself to furnish for publication "Guiteau's Married Life." Her narrative is in the sensational style, and no doubt she was well paid for it.

In 1869, after a short acquaintance and ten-hour notice, I

foolishly married this woman! I met her at the Y.M.C. Association, of Chicago, where she was employed as librarian. She came from Philadelphia, where she had been seduced, and had a child by a young blood —a married man. I had no business and no money at that time. I was not in any way prepared to take care of a wife. She was a poor, uneducated girl without position or friends, and about the last person for me to have married. She was very thin and delicate in appearance; stupid and stubborn in disposition, and our marriage was most unfortunate. As soon as I was married I opened a law office in Chicago and made about two thousand dollars that year. We always lived and dressed well; but we never lived together a week without having a serious quarrel. After four years of this experience I made up my mind I would sever the bond, and we were divorced, much to my satisfaction, in 1874. Since then I have known little about her, and care nothing, save to wish her well. Her narrative contains much that is false, but it is not worth my notice to correct it in detail. We were divorced without issue. I have been strictly virtuous for six or eight years, and have not dissipated in any way.

MY ACTIONS VINDICATED

A New York daily paper talks thus about a war prevented by Garfield's removal, which I herewith annex, as showing the drift of public sentiment:

Brief as the Garfield administration was, every week brings to light some new scandal which had its origin in the busy, scheming brain of the Secretary of State. A few days ago we laughed at Guiteau's pretense that his bullet had saved the country from a war, and yet today, we have the proofs that at the time President Garfield died a war was imminent. It was not the kind of war which was predicted but it was a war which could not have failed to be even more disastrous. If Mr. Blaine had had his way, instead of the profound peace which we now enjoy, the call to arms would be heard, and our shipyards would be busy on both shores of the continent fitting out a fleet to carry an army of occupation to the soil of a sister republic. ...

Never before in the history of the Republic was there such a Quixotic politician at the head of the Government. His schemes were reckless and daring, while his policy was guided neither by common sense nor common honesty. No sentiment, either of humanity or of duty, could reach him, and even while he stood by the bedside of his dying chief, he was plotting to embroil his country in a war, whose only result could be to benefit the corrupt rings of which he is the chief.

Even for a country as rich and as strong as the United States a war with Chili was an undertaking of no small magnitude. An army would have had to be conveyed a long distance, and it would have been necessary to create both an army and a navy. Alone, Chili would have been more of a match for us than the thirteen colonies were for Great Britain in 1776. But in this contest Chili would not have been alone. Both England and France could scarcely have refrained from taking a hand in the fight. All the world, except Peru, would have been against us, and in such a contest Peru would have been a very poor second. For once we would have met our match, and it requires no great foresight to perceive that we should have come out of it impoverished, shattered, and perhaps dismembered.

... We now see that Guiteau's bullet saved the country from a very grave danger, which could only have ended in a desolating war. The President, it is only too plain, was putty in the hands of his scheming Secretary. Blaine was bent upon a scheme, boldly conceived and craftily planned, out of which the roll of drums and the roar of cannon and the clash of arms would have been sure to come. It was to be a war of occupation and conquest, and it was at variance with a long-settled policy of the Republic and our notions of national and international polity.

The same newspaper in a later editorial talks thus:

Shall we come to the conclusion that seems forced upon us—that Guiteau was really inspired?

When he felt the Divine pressure upon him which compelled him to remove President Garfield to avert a bloody war, he could not have seen, except through the eye of inspired vision, that a war was really imminent. That he was mistaken in its character is not remarkable, for it is not always given, even to prophets, to see clearly the foreknowledge of the Lord. Be all this as it may, it is now certain that the effect of his act, as he proclaimed it in court, was practically to avert what he said it had averted. ... While Guiteau was on trial we saw no reason why a God, who interests Himself in the affairs of men, should wish to reverse His action at Chicago in June and at the polls in November, 1880. We are now compelled to admit that even a God who was willing to elect Garfield President of the United States could not foresee the wickedness of Blaine as Secretary of State. It might somehow be necessary that Guiteau should wear the mantle of inspiration in order to undermine the designs of the Mephistopheles who obtained power in consequence of a well-intended act of Providence.

A calm consideration of Blaine's wickedness in his projected war with Chili is almost impossible. It was to have been undertaken at a great cost of blood and treasure, only to assure possession of a guano heap and make a private speculation profitable. It was a cunning and crafty scheme, by which a few men were to make money by the sacrifice of many lives. Shudder as we may at Guiteau's act, it was his inspiration which prevented the success of the crime which Blaine contemplated without any pretense of inspiration.

In view of the revelations of the last few days, who can deny that it was the sacrifice of one life which saved the lives of thousands and perhaps the safety and perpetuity of the Republic itself?

Reasoning Mania

I condense the following from the New York *Herald* March 2, 1882:

> Reasoning Mania—Guiteau's case Analyzed.
>
> A full attendance of the Medico-Legal Society was present at the monthly meeting Last evening in the rooms on Thirty-first street. Dr. Charles S. Wood presided, and introduced Dr. Hammond, who read a paper on "Reasoning Mania; its Medical and Medico-Legal Relations, with Special Reference to the case of Charles Guiteau." The doctor passed around among the members a plaster cast of the head of Guiteau taken by order of the Government.
>
> The paper read by the doctor produced a powerful impression, and was listened to with the profoundest interest, being heartily applauded at the end. The doctor traced the first scientific attempts to treat reasoning mania by Pliny in 1801, and later on by Esquirol and by the younger Pliny, who called the affection "Mania of Character." After referring to the symptoms of the victims of the disease as given by these distinguished French writers, who were the first to differentiate the affection, the existence of which had also been affirmed by the best English and German alienists, such as Prichard, Connolly, Bucknillard, Maudsley and Hoffbauer, Caspar, Griesinger, Liman, and Kraft-Ebing. Dr. Hammond gave his own view of its characteristics.
>
> Among other things Dr. Hammond said:
>
> As to derangement of the intellect, I am quite sure that, though the emotions and the will are primarily and chiefly involved, there is more or less aberration of the purely intellectual faculties in every case of reasoning mania. Certainly this has been so in every instance that has come under my observation. To a superficial examination the intellect may appear to be unaffected, as it very generally happens that there is an absence of marked delusion. But a ready susceptibility to be im-

pressed by slight exciting causes; an unquestioning faith in their own powers, when in reality these are far below the average, and an entire disregard of their duties and obligations and of the ordinary proprieties of life, are certainly indications of intellectual derangement.

Applying the foregoing to Guiteau, and considering the manner in which he conducted himself while being tried for his life, his abuse of his friends who were endeavoring to save him, his praise of judge and jury and opposing counsel at one time, and his fierce denunciation of them at another, his speech in his defense, his entire lack of appreciation of the circumstances surrounding him, his evident misapprehension of the feelings of the people toward him, his belief in the intercession of prominent persons in his behalf and of his eventual triumph, and the many other indications with which you are all familiar, especially, his conduct after sentence was pronounced, I have no hesitation in asserting that Guiteau is the subject of reasoning mania, and hence a lunatic. There is not an asylum under the charge of any one of the medical experts for the prosecution that does not contain patients less insane than he. The emotional philosophers, desiring him to be sane, still endeavor to persuade themselves that their wishes and facts are the same thing, and, to the disgrace of American psychological medicine: they are sustained by certain physicians who appeared as witnesses for the prosecution. To shut our eyes to his exact condition and to try to flatter ourselves that he was of normally constituted mind when he shot the President, is not only cowardly; but it is impolitic. The conviction and execution will be without the force of an example upon hundreds of others of unsound minds, who may be contemplating the commission of crimes. And it will lead to the erroneous conclusion that there was a sane man, a man in the full possession of his mental faculties, capable of killing the President of the United States for the purpose of uniting the two wings of the Republican Party. Was there ever a more insane motive than this, and was there ever a man whose whole career, from childhood to the present day, has afforded a more striking example of that form of mental derangement called reasoning mania?

When the doctor concluded the chair called on Dr. Ralph L. Parsons to open the discussion on the paper just read. Dr. Parsons said he was long of the opinion that this paper was entirely correct. The characterization of this Guiteau form of insanity," he said, "places it equally strong on the basis of any other kind of insanity."

Dr. Spitzka said that there was a prevailing delusion that an expert in insanity had a profound knowledge of pathology, physiology, metaphysics, and many other things, but that was knocked on the head at Washington. He examined Guiteau before he testified, and he found that he was full of hallucinations. He wanted the mission to Austria and couldn't speak a word of German, and the mission to France, when he could not speak French. He believed he was doing a great act for the benefit of the American people. The form of insanity from which he is suffering is a German one and is equal to original insanity.

Dr. Barry said he agreed a good deal with the last speaker and with much that Dr. Hammond said. He thought it was impossible to have any line of demarcation between the moral and intellectual faculties. He made some amusing allusions to the Guiteau trial, and said he knew some of the inside workings, and was in the caucus of the prosecution. Guiteau was put through after the way they kill hogs in Chicago! No matter how the hog went in at one end of a cylinder, he came out at the other still a hog. The prosecution was determined Guiteau should come out the way they wanted, and they succeeded.

Dr. Mann said he was surprised at the position the experts took on the Guiteau trial. The form of Guiteau's insanity was theomania, and, if he lived, it would develop in melancholic mania or perhaps suicide. He was clearly insane, as Dr. Hammond says.

Dr. Gray, of Brooklyn, said that every case like Guiteau's, of proved in sanity, should be sent to a lunatic asylum, as the hanging of such a man would not deter others from following his example.

Dr. Sayre said the experts should have made the examination of Guiteau before the trial came off, and if found insane by a body of expert doctors he should be sent for life to a lunatic asylum, and the Government would be spared expense and scandal, and it would not go forth to the world that a sane man had murdered the President.

LETTERS FROM MY SUPPORTERS

My mail is received daily. I herewith attach some letters. I withhold the names and sometimes the place.

FROM MASSACHUSETTS—STICK TO GOD.
Boston, *Jan.* 23, 1882.

Sir: Pardon me if I send you a few words of greeting, as the hour draws near in which your fate is to be sealed. I have listened to the oratory and eloquence of Davidge and Porter, as well as the plea of your own counsel, and I can find nothing so logical in all those 1,000 pages of words, as I find in your few words to the honorable court, as follows: "If the jury believes that I believed it was right for me to remove the President, because I had special divine authority so to do, they will acquit on the ground of transitory mania." You have the whole thing in a nut-shell. It don't make any difference how sane you are today, or was a year ago or less. Was you faithful to yourself the 2nd of July? For fidelity to one's self is all the standard there is to right and wrong. Right as you see it, truth as you see it, duty as you see it, though not perhaps as others see it. We do not all see God alike. We do not all hear Him alike. We do not all worship Him alike.

I am looking out from my window upon the scraggy lines of an elm tree, surrounded by the statues of Charles Sumner, Edward Everett, Daniel Webster, and Horace Mann. This tree was the chosen one for the judicial murder of four persons. What had they done? They were exiled Quakers who had returned to Boston. Mary Dyer, a woman, when led up to this tree, was offered her life if she would go away; or, in other words, if she would hear that still small voice as her persecutors did. But no. She said, "I hear a voice you cannot hear, that says I must not stay away. I see a finger you cannot see, that points me the way. Which shall I obey? Nay; in obedience to the will of the Lord I came, and in His will I will abide faithful to, death." And she offered her neck to

136

the rope. What Christian minister today commends that fiendish act? Is God dead? Can no one see or hear Him today, only in just such a way as may be pointed out to him by some melancholy fellow? Now, if God told you to shoot the President, stick to it. Who should know better than you? You touched the key-note in those few words you used in your plea. And if God be with you, who shall be against you? Though the American States may hang your body, and the American church may damn your soul, whoever believes in progress will find a friend in Charles Guiteau.

FROM INDIANA—
THE SAVIOR OF YOUR COUNTRY.
Fort Wayne, Indiana, *Dec.* 30, 1881.

Dear Sir: I feel it my duty as a Christian to address you a few words of sympathy in your present unhappy situation. I do not see why this Government should put on its whole armor of power and use the whole U. S. Treasury in the attempt to convict you of a crime of which you are not guilty. You, nothing but the humble instrument of the "God who moves in a mysterious way His wonders to perform," to save our blessed land from destruction by the removal of Garfield, and by putting Arthur in his stead. You were the chosen one from among the faithful to do the will of the ever living God, and for you goes up prayers at early morn, noon, and night, to the throne of Him who doeth all things well, and who had predestined you from the cradle to be the second savior of your country; and every presbyter and their hearers will swell the prayers to Him who sent you. Fear not what the ungodly Corkhill and Porter may do, because the Lord is your shield and your strength, and His will be done as it was from the beginning. You were selected to save our party and through our party our country, and through our country our religion. The religion that was landed on Plymouth Rock.

FROM WISCONSIN—THE DEITY WILL KEEP YOU HARMLESS.
Eau Claire, Wis. *Jan.* 29, 1882.

You will please pardon the liberty I am taking in thus addressing you. I have been greatly interested in your trial throughout. You claim that your removing the President was by Divine inspiration. Do you not feet that the same power which inspired you to do the act will still watch over you and save you from harm? If you were only the instrument or means used to carry out a plan of Deity, then you are not responsible for the act. He who knoweth all thing's surely must have seen the end and have provided for all emergencies.

FROM OHIO—KING OF THE STALWARTS.
Hon. Charles Guiteau:

> I am only a maid of Ohio's parts,
> And you are King of the Stalwarts;
> But will you be so kind in my behalf,
> As to favor me with your autograph?

FROM TENNESSEE—WANTS ME FOR PRESIDENT.
Knoxville, Tenn. *Dec.* 30, 1881.

Dear Sir: Allow us to express our unbounded admiration for you. We second the motion to nominate you for President.

FROM THE OLD DOMINION—STAND TO YOUR COLORS.
Norfolk, *Jan.* 13, 1882.
Hon. **Charles Guiteau:**

The Stalwarts of the Old Dominion send you greeting and wish you the best future. Stand to your colors. Warm up old Corkhill. Let the world know that true pat-

138

riotism is not dead in America yet.

In the envelope containing the above letter this was enclosed:

Jan. 13, 1882.
Mr. Guiteau:

You have the fullest sympathy of our community and we consider you one of the greatest and most intellectual men of the day, and think you have treated Corkhill exactly right for the sneaking way he has treated you, and we are confident of your ability to come out all right, as we are fully confident of your inspiration.

FROM ILLINOIS—SUSTAINED BY DIVINITY.

I deeply deplore your pending doom. Will money assist you any now? Being a widow left with much property, I would willingly help you. There surely could be no better way to invest a thousand, or two, than to help a fellow mortal condemned by man but sustained by divinity.

Please send me a lock of your hair as a memento of the man who was brave enough to sacrifice his life for his beloved party.

FROM NEW YORK—FINAL SUCCESS SURE.

New York, *Feb.* 1, 1882.
The Honorable Charles Guiteau:

Dear Sir: Will you kindly grant me the favor of possessing your autograph, and adding it to those of other illustrious men. I have been a close observer of your struggle with Porter, and although victory appears now with the Government, I think your final success is beyond all question. With profound respect for the manly course your have pursued, I remain

Faithfully yours,

HANG THE DEITY IF ANYBODY.
Charles Guiteau:

Your inspiration is characterized by the prosecution as irreverent and blasphemous. That repudiates the idea of inspiration. If the jury concurs in that view, they then declare that there is no Divine inspiration. If that be their verdict it repudiates the Bible. "believed to be the inspired book of men."

If, on the other hand, they decide that you were inspired by God, you can only have been the instrument in His hands, "an accessory to the killing, and the principal being known He should be held responsible." Let them hang the Deity if anybody.

FROM DELAWARE—EYES FILLED WITH TEARS.
Frederica, *Jan.* 9, 1882.

Dear Sir: I have been reading the papers and very truly sympathize with you. There were great arguments on the subject from the people of this town, but now, when the news is a little contrary, their eyes fill with tears. They will be happy to hear of your acquittal, but be of good cheer; the Savior will be with you.

A FRENCH-CANADIAN—TO ADMIRE YOU I DO NOT LEAVE OFF..
Repentigny, *Jan.* 3rd. 1882.

Dear Sir: As a French-Canadian, I must tell you that I sympathize very much with you, and that to admire you I do not leave off.

FROM CANADA—A NEW TRIAL WILL GIVE AN ACQUITTAL.
Toronto, 10 *Feb.* 1882.

Dear Sir: If you think there is any likelihood of the

court granting a new trial, and you are in need of funds to employ good counsel, I shall be glad to forward you a draft for a substantial amount upon hearing from you. I heartily sympathize with you, and consider that another trial would convince the jury of your innocence.

FROM A PENNSYLVANIA STALWART.

Harrisburg, *Dec.* 31, 1881.
To the Hon. Charles Guiteau:

When on the 2nd day of July I heard of the assassination of "President Garfield," I thought the crime horrible, and also thought the hangman's noose too good for you, but now, since the trial has thrown light on the case, I, too, believe in your much-talked-of "inspiration."

I have consulted with many of my brother "Stalwarts," and they, too, believe that the removal of "President Garfield" was committed by you through a direct inspiration. We earnestly hope that the "court" will see it in the same light that you and ourselves see it, because if the jury should render a verdict of "guilty." it would be a stigma on the rights of justice and liberty.

The prophecies you made at the time of the assassination have all come true. Peace and harmony reigns within the party. Keep up good cheer, and you will come through safe.

FROM MASSACHUSETTS—MIRACLES ARE NOT YET ENDED.

Don't despair, even if you are brought to the very foot of the gallows. A thunderbolt will crush your enemies and release you. Miracles are not yet ended, and such a man as you will be preserved, even if the very heavens should fall to do it.

FROM BOSTON—DENOUNCING THE GALLOWS.

Boston, *Dec.* **30, 1881.**
Charles Guiteau:

Dear Sir: The most hateful and damnable of all crimes and cruelties ever perpetrated upon the face of the earth or in the regions of hell is that of capital punishment; and the man who takes the life of a fellow-man in the cold blood of the law must have the germ of the very devil in his heart, or he would revolt from it. It is a Christian impulse and a Christian's duty to abhor such a monster as one would the very arch-fiend himself.

FROM MINNESOTA—HOPING I WILL BE PARDONED.

Charles Guiteau, Esq. *Washington:*

Enclosed find check for fifty dollars. Rest assured I sympathize with you, and only trust you may be pardoned by our good President.

And this moves me to say, should I desire President Arthur to pardon me, I will make a formal requisition on him under my own hand. I make this announcement that irresponsible persons may not annoy the President or me.

FROM A MINISTER.

Boston, *March* **2, 1882.**
Charles Guiteau:

Dear Sir: I have long admired you for your honesty of purpose and your true Christian character. I am an earnest believer in your innocence; that is, that you were not responsible for the shot that killed President Garfield. I wish that I could have your autograph, that it might be handed down to my children and my children's children.

Yours, with great respect,

FROM MARYLAND.

Baltimore, *February* 8, 1882.

My **Dear Sir:** The news of your misfortune has deeply afflicted many. Who can foretell what may happen the next moment? But it is not my intentions to increase your painful feelings by my lamentations. Your misfortune is no fault of your own. This should mitigate your grief and keep up your spirits. Take courage; when night is darkest dawn is nearest.

FROM MASSACHUSETTS.

Boston, *Jan.* 30, 1882.
Mr. Guiteau:

Dear Sir: Having been found among the most ardent admirers of your courage, fortitude, and self-reliance during the days of the recent trial, we (my sister and myself) have at last found courage to pen these few lines, begging the honor and pleasure of your correspondence, or at least a few lines from you as a memento of one who was willing to risk his life or liberty for the benefit of his loved but ungrateful country.

From your sympathizing friends,

LAURA and EVA.

FROM KANSAS—"GUITEAU THE GREAT."

Charles Guiteau:

My **Dear** Sir: Being a poor boy, and knowing (as but few seem to appreciate) your kind and benevolent disposition, I beg of you to send me your photograph and autograph, and I promise you that this Western country will hear from your good deeds. Yes, and it will help to bring to light your real character. I know, though you be "Guiteau the Great," you will *ever* be *generous* and not forget the poor.

Believe me your humble servant,

P. S.—The reason I want your photo is to remember the greatest of Americans and to let the people here see your good face.

FROM NEW YORK—KEEP UP COURAGE.

Sir: We have watched with intense interest the course of the great trial in which you have borne so important a part, and must congratulate you upon your heroic behavior through it all; and, although our sympathies are with you in your defeat this time, yet success may attend your efforts, if the Lord be with you, in gaining a new trial; and all may yet be well if you keep up good courage, as you certainly must, as herein lies the victory.

FROM OHIO.

Hamilton, O. *Feb.* **4, 1882.**
Charles Guiteau. *Washington, D.C.:*

Dear Sir: Accept my sympathy with you in your hour of misfortune. The darkest cloud has its "silver lining."

FROM PENNSYLVANIA.

West Chester, Pa. *Dec.* **31, 1881.**
Charles Guiteau, Esq.:

Dear Sir: The people here are all reading your trial proceeding with much interest, Glad that you keep up such courage. We all wish you success in '84. And if you should run, look out for a big vote from this section. People of West Chester sympathize with you.

FROM VIRGINIA.

Lexington, Va., *Jan.* **2, 1882.**
Charles Guiteau:

The whole town is in sympathy with you. We propose to run you in the convention of 1884 for President, and think that you are a smart man, and always have thought that you ought to be President.

FROM MASSACHUSETTS.
Belchertown, Mass. *Dec.* **31, 1881.**
Hon. Charles Guiteau:

Realizing the fact that the name of Charles Guiteau will stand as one of the great names in American history, I should consider it an honor to be the possessor of his autograph.

FROM DAKOTA.
Vermillion, Dakota, *Jan.* **28, 1882.**
Hon. Charles Guiteau:

I am a little girl living on the wild prairies of Dakota. I am making a collection of autographs for my album. Will you favor me with yours? I should prize it highly.

FROM CALIFORNIA.
San Francisco, *Jan.* **27, 1882.**
Charles Guiteau:

Dear Sir: I take this method of offering to you my sympathy, and desire to extend to you any courtesy that I can. The people of San Francisco are with you, and desire you to write to our press. I ask you most humbly to give me as a memento (of so great a man) your autograph.

FROM MASSACHUSETTS—TRUST IN GOD.
Charles Guiteau, Esq.:

Dear Sir: I should be very much pleased if you would be kind enough to send me your autograph, which I should prize highly. I have much sympathy for you in your unfortunate position, and beg you to place your trust in God, who doeth all things well.

FROM OHIO.
Charles Guiteau:

My friend in Jesus Christ: I am praying to God that this nation will absolve you for shooting President Garfield, when you were a lunatic. You have been a madman on religion; that is a fact which cannot be disputed.

FROM BUFFALO, NEW YORK.
Charles Guiteau, Esq'r:

Sir: I have watched the trial ever since it commenced, and have come to the conclusion that there is not another man in America that could fill your boots. I want your handwriting to put into my collection, as I have letters from the following great men:
John Wesley.
Duke of Wellington.
Lord Brougham.
Lord Aberdeen.
Lord Dungannon.
Daniel O'Connell.
Adam Clark.
And many other great men.

FROM KENTUCKY—A FOOLISH VERDICT.
Charles Guiteau:

Dear Sir: I, with many others, have watched with intense anxiety your recent trial, and sincerely deplore the unexpected and foolish verdict that has been rendered. We admire you for the pluck displayed during your severe ordeal, and beg of you to be of good cheer as you will surely receive a new trial, when your *true* character will be shown and you will be vindicated, not only before the eyes of the American people, but of the whole world. This nation will yet bless you for the noble deed you have performed. With many wishes for your long life and prosperity, I remain yours truly,.

FROM ALABAMA.

Selma, Ala. *Jan.* 10, 1882.
Charles Guiteau:

Your time has *not* come. The Lord is with you as well as are all liberal-minded men outside the court-room. Do not despair.

You have well succeeded in entertaining the world for the last few weeks. May your wit never grow dull, nor your shadow less.

FROM INDIANA—SHALL MAN OPPOSE HIMSELF TO GOD'S WILL?

These sentiments are from an Indiana paper. It was sent me in a letter:

"Brother Arthur says his illustrious predecessor was removed by the mysterious will of the Almighty. In this he agrees with Guiteau. And why, if Guiteau is insane, isn't Brother Arthur insane? They agree that it was God's will that Garfield should be 'removed.' And shall we oppose ourselves to God's ' will?' Shall man set himself up against God? Shall man set himself up against the humble instrument employed by God to execute His will? Are we not laying the hand of the law upon Guiteau at our peril? Shouldn't he rather be canonized as a saint than hung as an assassin? Short-sighted man! be careful how you raise your puny hand against the will of God."

FROM A MEMBER OF THE IOWA ASSEMBLY.
January 4, 1882.
Charles Guiteau: *Washington, D.C.:*

Dear Sir: The people of this vicinity earnestly hope that the fact of your inspiration will be proven.

The American people are fast seeing that your act is proving itself to be the most beneficial to the Republican Party.

FROM COLORADO—A MAN OF BRAINS.
Colorado Springs, *Jan.* 9, 1882.
Hon. Charles Guiteau:

Dear Sir: I was much surprised to hear that you were placed in the prisoner's dock. I think it an act of tyranny on the part of the court, as you were acting as your own counsel.

Your trial is eagerly read, and people are looking for your release, believing that you have the best side of the case. No one believes you to be a crank. Your remarks in court show that you are a man of good brains, and you would stand a good show as candidate for senator- ship of Colorado, or even for the Presidency of the United States. You are spoken of a great deal here, and many have expressed a desire to read your book on "Truth."

FROM MAINE—
"TO THE PLUCKIEST MAN IN AMERICA."
West Paris, *Jan.* 1, 1882.
Charles Guiteau, Esq.:

The pluckiest man in America! I would like your autograph for my album with such a sentiment as you might be pleased to write.

I send envelope, stamped addressed, with New Year's greetings.

From your little friend,

Miss _____ ,

A 13 year-old School Girl.

I would send you money for your photograph if you had any to spare.

FROM INDIANA—CAN MEN OVERPOWER GOD?

Albany, Indiana, *Jan.* **31, 1882.**
Hon. Charles Guiteau, *Washington, D.C.:*

In response to your appeal to the ladies of the Government, of which you are the deliverer, I humbly beg you to accept all I am able to offer—a letter of sympathy and a woman's love. It was with the highest degree of fervor I read your appeal for aid, and I sincerely regret that I cannot offer even a small sum; but I hope and firmly believe that your call will be answered and abundant means furnished to employ for you an army of legal talent. I was truly surprised to learn that a body of twelve men selected from an enlightened (?) city should return such an unwarranted verdict. Did they not counteract God's will? Do they not oppose divine rule? Will not the meagre district court be held accountable for countermanding the order of that Judge whose bench Judge Cox, the jury, and prosecution may never see? All these things are being considered by the thinking world. It is true that the judge on the bench and the jury in the box, influenced by the mercenary efforts of the unprincipled Corkhill and the truculent Porter. hold that you are a guilty murderer, and claim the authority to deprive you of your valuable life; but was it murder? Are you to be held accountable for an act planned by the Deity, who only made you a helpless instrument to save the nation? Is it not a supreme honor to be God's agent? Think not for a moment that this murderous decision will be executed. Can men overpower God? Have they not tried it and failed? Has not God protected you in the past and given assurance that he would in future? Besides, public opinion is so rapidly favoring you that ere the sentence can be executed the people will demand your release, and your honors will be unprecedented. I know what I say, and am now only expressing what myriads of people (especially my sex) endorse.

To the future nation's pride. Charles Guiteau.

FROM DENMARK.
Copenhagen, Denmark, the 15 *Feb.* 1882.

Sir: I am a Danish student, but as I fear that you don't understand the language of my country, I shall try to express my thoughts in the English language.

In the last year every man in the world has known Sir Charles Guiteau; even in my little beautiful country your name has been upon all lips; some admire you, some fear you.

As I am a collector of autographies, I should be very happy if you would do me the favor to send me a few words from your own hand.

FROM ENGLAND.
Feb. 21, 1882.

Dear Sir: You would confer a great favor upon me if you would only be so kind as to send me your autograph, a writing I should value above all things. If you should be kind enough to grant my request, would you only write your name on a slip of paper and put it in the envelope which I enclose, and send it to me.

Hoping that you will look with favor upon my demand, and with kindest wishes, believe me—

FROM NEW YORK—A GREAT POLITICAL WRONG.
Brooklyn, *Feb.* 17, 1882.
The Honorable Charles Guiteau:

As an admirer of your character, and as a sympathizer with you under the great injustice you have suffered, I should esteem it a great favor to possess some slight memorial of you. Will you kindly favor me with a verse or line on the enclosed, authenticated by your autograph, which it will be my pride and pleasure to religiously keep all my life and hand to my children as a memento of a great political wrong.

Wishing you every happiness and the support of that God on whom you ever relied in your hour of great affliction, I am, dear sir, your sincere well wisher and admirer.

FROM WISCONSIN—I DID RIGHT TO REMOVE THE PRESIDENT.
Eau Claire, *Feb.* **15, 1882.**
Charles Guiteau:

Dear Sir: You do not know how many ladies there are here who believe that you did right to remove the President. I am one of them, and I believe your name will be one of the brightest in our history or in the history of any other nation. I hope you will have a new trial and the court in banc will reverse the decision. I hope you will answer this in your own hand as I wish to preserve your autograph as a memento of a great man.

FROM MINNESOTA—THINKS I WILL COME OUT ALL RIGHT.
Minneapolis, Minn. 2-18, 1882.
Charles Guiteau:

Dear Sir: Allow me to express my most heartfelt sympathy for you. I hope you have the confidence in God the papers claim you have. I think you will come out all right yet.

FROM MAINE—SAYS I OUGHT TO BE RELEASED.
Charles Guiteau, Esq.:

There is a strong feeling here in the Eastward among nearly all classes in favor of your release. Wishing that your name, which must live centuries after the names of your accusers have been forgotten, and yourself may long be spared the country you have really saved. I am yours respectfully,

FROM MISSOURI.
Hon. Charles Guiteau:

Please accept the heart-felt sympathy of friends in Missouri. From the first you have claimed the sympathy of some friends at least. Our nation mourns the loss of a good President, but our sympathy for him and his family must not cause us to forget that there are others who need our sympathizing prayers.

FROM MICHIGAN—"A STALWART OF THE STALWARTS."
Hon. Chas. Guiteau, *Washington, D.C.:*

Those fellows are not doing right by you. You are a stalwart of the Stalwarts, and anything I can do in my power to help you, I will be pleased to do. Let me know if you need any help in the way of money or political influence.

FROM TEN SCHOOL CHILDREN—BOYS AND GIRLS—IN MICHIGAN.
Mr. Guiteau:

We, the scholars of a school in the interior of Michigan, which to express by letter our sympathy for you.

Your name has become familiar to every child, and when it goes down in history you will appear in a different light than that in which you are now represented to the public. The minds of the people, cleared of prejudice or passion, will then consider you in your true character. As it is now, the press of the United States has so involved and misconstrued your actions that your life presents one continued mesh of contradictions. Hoping that one day or other you will stand on your merits in the estimation of the people, we very respectfully solicit an answer to this expression of sympathy.

FROM ILLINOIS—THINKS I AM "A GREATER MAN THAN GRANT, LINCOLN, OR WASHINGTON."

Chicago, *Jan.* **2, 1882.**
Charles Guiteau, Esq.:

Honored Sir: The majority of the American people are beginning to see your case in its true light. I would buy your photograph in preference to Garfield's any day, and so would a great many other people. They are beginning to think of you as a greater man than Grant, Lincoln, or Washington.

FROM A DISTINGUISHED MINISTER OF NEW YORK.

New York, *Jan.* **14, 1882.**
Charles Guiteau, *Washington, D.C.:*

Dear Sir: Put your trust in God and you will come out triumphantly in the end. I am satisfied that you are an innocent and much abused man, but don't let your courage fail you. Everything will be all right. Keep up good cheer.

Yours, very truly,
Rev. _____ .

FROM ENGLAND.

England, *Jan.* **23, 1882.**

Dear Sir: The world at large—England especially— looks first with longing eyes each morning for the latest words which have fallen from your mouth. Your name will be handed down to posterity. By sending me two separate autographs of yours, which, when obtained, will be placed amongst those of other great men, you will confer a great favor upon yours, truly.

FROM A PHILADELPHIA LAWYER—NO MALICE IN THIS CASE; THEREFORE NO CRIME.

January 1, 1882.

Sir: If you don't hang the jury someway it will be apt to hang you. You would be in no danger if the jurymen and the judge were all thinkers and philosophers, but they are not. They are frail mortals, and will be apt to fall in with the morbid clamor for your blood. Corkhill is an ass and cannot appreciate the fine point on which your case turns. Porter is a brute, and cares for nothing but his fee. Davidge is playing *soupe* in the farce of a prosecution, and like all who play subordinate parts falls in with any nonsense the others adopt. Judge Cox is a good kind of a creature, but with no ability or learning. Scoville is doing as well for your defense as a routine attorney could be expected, but he has been stumbling along where angels fear to tread, and where he has hit the essential matter in your case it has been by accident rather than design.

You have made the only point and stuck to it all through this long trial, that can be made, and that is where there is no malice there can be no crime. Every murder is a killing; but every killing is not murder. If you were sane on the 2nd of July last you had no conceivable motive of malice for shooting the President.

If you were not sane, of course you are not responsible in law. If you have that total depravity of heart, fatally bent on mischief, which Blackstone describes as implied malice in law, it is strange that it should never before have been exhibited in your life. The facts brought out by the prosecution about your supposed dishonest transactions in business affairs do not establish the wickedness of heart which produces malice in law to

154

convict of murder. If you have that kind of malice it would have appeared long ago in murdering other people, or in attempts to murder them. There was no actual malice, for this must have a motive, on which mankind usually acts in such cases. They can't call it revenge for refusing to appoint you to office for you had not been finally refused, but only put off, as many are who are finally appointed. Hayes used to reject men whom he finally appointed, and appointed men whom he told he never could appoint. Garfield and Blaine were counterparts of Hayes in prominent traits of character. People have wondered how Hayes ever got through his term of lying and hypocrisy without meeting a Guiteau who had a real motive for personal violence. Garfield, if he possessed the same traits of character as most people who were acquainted with him believe, had not so far developed it when you shot him as to afford the slightest justification for your act. Garfield had a better heart than Hayes, but he was weak and vacillating. He had ability of high order and much book-learning, but no balance and no common sense. He would have proved a perfect failure as President, but that was no reason why he should have been killed either by you or the doctors. And if all they claim to have proved about you were true, Garfield would have been as apt to appoint you as anybody. He made some appointments no less amazing; so that you had as much right to anticipate honors from him, cranky and dishonest as they claim you are, as many others who succeeded in their importunities. I think, therefore, you tell the truth when you say that it was not from ill-will, growing out of disappointment, that caused you to shoot the President.

Your lawyers call it insanity; you call it a "pressure" from the Deity to do an act which the Divine wisdom thought ought to be done for the good of the country; of which of course you must be the judge in the first instance, as no other man could be a judge for you; I mean as to the "inspiration." When Moses had an inspiration to retire to the smoking mountain of Sinai to write the tables for the Israelites, he didn't receive an intimation of it from anybody else, and he didn't have to "prove" it to the satisfaction of any captive Jews. He felt it and acted upon it, and the *result* showed he was not an imposter. The same may be said of the Apostles. Paul's own statement has always been taken, and the Scripture is based on it so far as he is concerned, when he told how he became converted and what "pressure" was brought on him to change his course of life, and how God inspired his writing and preaching. If there is a God and our religion is not a lie, as the crank Ingersoll declares, that same Deity which knows no variableness or shadow of turning can select His instruments, now as well as then.

But it makes no practical difference whether you are right or Scoville is right in the pith of the matter. It is not murder in any case. If it was a *real* inspiration, there was no more reason to call you insane than to call Moses, the Prophets, and the Apostles insane. But as we must have civil administration as well as divine in human governments, all *sons* of men must in the first instance be held responsible for their acts which are forbidden by law and let the Almighty take care of the rest. When God moves in one direction and man in another, conflicts become mysterious and irreconcilable to our narrow views. Individuals must perish in this seeming conflict, but God's wisdom will be vindicated at last. And as a matter of fact we find there never has been any punishment in such cases as yours. Christ had to be crucified according to the divine economy, and the irresponsible mob of Jews who crucified him were technically guilty of homicide under the law of the land, but as a fact they were never punished. When Stephen was stoned to death it was murder, but not only did the murderer escape, but Stephen himself asked that he be forgiven, as Christ had said of his murderers, "Father, forgive them, for they know not what they do." Supposing you to have been sane, your act will stand out in history in the same category, and roll down the ages for a divine purpose. If it was an "insane delusion" of your own. without an inspiration, of course you cannot be convicted. Still less, if you, as a matter of fact, have never been a sane man. But if your act has more of the ingredients of murder, as you can demonstrate if you understood your own case, it makes no difference, as I have said, what defense is put in. Garfield fell a victim to influences and circumstances which he helped to bring about. The moral world is governed by laws as certain as those of the physical. You might as well say God is guilty of murder when His lightning strikes and kills as to say you are guilty, when you conducted against the person of the President the fatal surcharge of the political atmosphere on the 2nd of July. Brutus committed technical homicide when he stabbed Caesar in the senate-house instead of a railroad depot, but his act was never regarded as criminal, but historical, for which we of America applaud him. He didn't love Caesar less, but Rome more. Charlotte Corday committed assassination when she slew Murat in a bath-tub, but she was not punished because she executed, if not the will of God, the known will of the people of France. Killing a king or sovereign is treason, not murder, in the old world; and the truth is *we have no law on the subject.* If they convict you for killing the *man* Garfield they will do so without showing the least motive for the act, and by upsetting the whole theory and precedents of the common law.

FROM IOWA—AN OFFER OF MARRIAGE.

I am in receipt of this letter dated March 10, 1882:

Mr. Guiteau:

    Dear Friend: I have read all about you in the papers. We all sympathize with you out in this country, and hope you will get out all right. I don't believe you will be hung. Now, will you please send me your photograph? I would like to have it very much. Enclosed you will find mine. I am 19 years old, and very good looking. I am rich and want a husband. If you think I would suit you, please let me know.

ATTEMPTS ON MY LIFE

THRICE SAVED FROM DEATH.

I hereby record that I adore the Almighty Father and the Savior for the kind providence that has been with me all my life, and especially since I have been in jail. Thrice I have been shot at and missed since July 2. The most providential escape from death was by Mason's bullet. It passed within an inch of my head and left my profile on the lead. Jones' bullet grazed my arm, but it did me no harm. A guard in the jail placed his pistol within six inches of my head in August, and I clinched him and held him until relieved by friendly guards. In the scuffle he fired his pistol at my head, but it missed me. I record this experience as acts of the Deity in my favor.

MASON.

From the Washington *Post* March 14, 1882:

> From being-over loquacious Guiteau has gravitated to the other extreme, and now opens his mouth only at rare and stated intervals. He heard of Mason's sentence late Sunday afternoon. Strange to say he made no comment upon it, not even showing by any act that he felt the slightest interest in Mason or any of his kin. He has since steadily refused to talk about the sentence, contenting himself with remarking, when pressed for his opinion: "O, well, I suppose if he intended to kill me, the sentence was all right"—a certainly intensely non-committal phrase. It is the opinion of those who have most closely observed him that he really casts no thoughts upon Mason, regarding him only as a wicked reed which was broken by divine power.

A New York paper, in discussing Mason's sentence, uses these words, which I endorse:

> This artilleryman struck a blow at the reputation of the regular troops for obedience to orders under all circumstances. To have punished him more lightly would have helped to spread the conviction that the troops could not be relied upon to perform disagreeable duty

in moments of great public excitement, and it would have half condoned one of the greatest offences which a soldier can be guilty of in time of peace.

MY LIFE IN JAIL.

[From the **Baltimore Sun,** March 6.]

Through the courtesy of Gen. Crocker, warden of the jail, a representative of *The Sun* was admitted to Guiteau's cell on Saturday. The prisoner has improved in appearance remarkably since his trial. His complexion is clear, and shows the glow of health and good living without excess. While upon close view there is a peculiarity in the expression of Guiteau's eye, it is not sufficiently noticeable to attract attention under ordinary circumstances. He wears a new suit of dark clothing, fresh linen, and a wide-brimmed soft hat, keeping the latter constantly upon his head, even in the presence of lady visitors. Two cells are at his disposal, one of which he uses as an office and the other as a sleeping apartment. The office is furnished with several chairs, a desk, and writing materials. The prisoner said he was well treated by everybody. He had numerous visitors, from whom he realized $25 to $30 per day by the sale of autographs and photographs. He exhibited four pictures in different positions, recently taken, saying he preferred those in which the face was turned to the side. These give the countenance an expression of severity not natural to it. The proceeds of this traffic afford him the means of supplying various comforts and the daily newspapers . Judging by the testimony on his trial of the shifts he has employed to get along in the past, he is in easier circumstances now than he has been for a long while. He reads pretty much all that is published about himself, and is very fond of fruit and buys a great deal of it. He disapproves of Mrs. Scoville's letters to Mrs. Garfield and President Arthur, and has notified her not to write any more letters in his behalf. In reference to his prospects, Guiteau said confidently: "We expect relief from the court in banc." He hoped Mr. Conkling would accept the seat on the Supreme Bench for the good of the country. Guiteau is anxious to have a new book published, which will contain a revision of his work on the

Bible, a sketch of his life, and an abstract of the trial. He is desirous that a Baltimore house should publish it, and says he is losing $50 a day while it remains unprinted. At parting the prisoner said: "I will give you a sentiment," and he wrote on a slip of paper the words, "The Republican Party—wrecked by Garfield; saved by Guiteau's inspiration and Arthur's statesmanship. Tell the readers of *The Sun* that I am well and happy, and have no apprehensions of any other condition either here or hereafter." His manner is entirely free from anything that would indicate that he did not feel as he spoke. He replies to all interrogations with promptness and decision, and speaks freely upon any topic introduced. When visitors appear at the door of his cell he invites them to enter, encouraging the timid with the assurance that he will not hurt them. He displays the air of a busy man of affairs, much in earnest and entirely sane, entertaining visitors as would become a man in the position of a host perfectly at ease.

PERSONAL.

As I have been terribly vilified by certain disreputable newspapers, and have had diabolical-looking pictures printed in some illustrated newspapers, pretending to represent my profile, I herewith give my personal appearance: Age, forty— am often taken for thirty; height, 5 feet 5 3/4 inches; weight, 140 pounds. Body compact and well built. Head, round and plump. Brains, let the public pass on that. Complexion, clear, light, and bright. Eyes, the same. Hair, brown; worn short. Face, clean, with a slight moustache. Manners, those of a high-toned Christian gentleman. Habits, I do not dissipate in any way. Health, excellent.

My time is pleasantly spent in reading, writing, and entertaining company. I have no anxiety about myself for this world or the next. The Lord always takes care of His man.

To Newspapers.

Certain newspaper cranks delight in the use of the words *"Guiteau the Assassin."* The word assassin is getting to be a high-toned word. Applied to me it sounds as well as the word "patriot."

Guiteau, the Patriot.

Guiteau, the Assassin.

Cranks can take their choice.

The most venomous men on the American press on this Guiteau-Garfield business are "Josef" Medill, of the *Chicago Tribune;* W. Reid, of the *New York Tribune;* M. Halstead, of the *Cincinnati Commercial;* and Curtis, the man-milliner of *Harper's Weekly.* These fellows are so badly cranked they will be in a lunatic asylum if they do not have a care. They should remember that Grant, Conkling, and Arthur elected Garfield and not they. I hereby invite them to join the Grant-Guiteau- Arthur Combination and behave themselves. I hereby notify them to hold their venom. Let them stop cursing God's man. If they cannot, let them follow the advice of Job's wife: "Curse God and die." Then the Almighty will get even with them for their diabolical spirit in this matter. The poodle dogs, of "the minor press," as Horace Greeley called the two-cent dailies, are hardly worth my notice. I pass them as a Fifth avenue gentleman would the bark of a cur.

THIS BOOK IS COPYRIGHTED.

By the statement in the preface, "that editors, not newspaper devils, may review this book," I mean that they will only be allowed to review it generally. I do not mean to destroy the copyright. No one has a right to copy any part of this book without special permission from me, as it is copyrighted. The public can buy it if they want it.

THE PRESIDENCY—
J.A.G., C.A.A., AND C.J.G.

Apropos to the Presidency, it has been discovered that the initials of Garfield, J.A.G. and Arthur, C.A.A. and Guiteau, C.J.G. intermingle mysteriously. Eliminate the letters common to each, *i.e.,* the A's, and it leaves C.J.G. To lovers of the mysterious this certainly is striking. These initials may, and probably do, indicate three Presidents, *i.e.,* three acts of the Deity.

MY SENTIMENT.

I close this book with this sentiment: The Republican Party, wrecked by Garfield, saved by Guiteau's inspiration and Arthur's statesmanship.

The political, financial, and social tranquility this nation to-day enjoys, all come from my inspiration in removing Garfield. Where would the Republican Party have been *today*, and what the condition of this nation had Garfield continued to run politics as he was doing last June? Let the cranks tell. They had better stop cursing God's man and commence to praise him.

I see the Lord is after Dr. Gray. He will probably send for the rest of my enemies soon. Beware, ye minions of the law, how ye treat me, lest ye kindle the wrath of the Deity and perish from the way! "Be instructed," says the Psalmist, "ye judges of the earth. Serve the Lord with fear, and rejoice with trembling. Kiss the Son lest He be angry, and ye perish from the way."

APPENDIX.

GARFIELD.

I INSERT the following from the Washington *Post* March 10, 1882. It is high time this Garfield gush was over. It is sickening to see what fools there are in this world. How some fools will curse a man living and deity him dead. If the men that were cursing Garfield last spring had any honor they would think of him now, as they did when he was wrecking the Republican Party and imperiling the life of the Republic. Let Garfield go into history with his true record, to wit: the President who wrecked the Republican Party and imperiled the happiness and life of this Nation:

To the Editor of the Post:

I read with great interest the Garfield-Chase letter in your paper today. I will take an oath it is genuine, for I saw the original in Mr. Chase's house in 1867, when he resided on the corner of Sixth and E streets. What became of it, and how it turns up now, I do not know. To one who knew Garfield well this letter is no surprise. He was a treacherous, a cowardly, a hypocritical man, selfish to the extreme, and not caring what happened, so it did not happen to himself. Gen. Rosecrans was and is worth to this country a thousand Garfields. When the fighting that Garfield was craving for came on he took good care to keep out of danger. It is high time, for the sake of our national common sense, the truth of history and justice alike to the living and the dead, that all this gush over Garfield should end. He was nothing but a professional office-seeker and politician! No one can point to an original thought he ever uttered. He betrayed John Sherman at Chicago as treacherously as Brutus did Caesar or Judas did Christ. No one wants to do injustice to a dead man, but they are worth no more than living ones, and living or dead the reputation of a brave, patriotic, and useful soldier like Gen. Rosecrans should not suffer in the eyes or thoughts of our people by the words of such a man as Garfield.

LETTERS FROM THE DAUGHTER OF A NEW YORK LAWYER.

I am in receipt of the following letters which I print as a part of my history. The author is the daughter of a New York lawyer. I withhold her name, as I print them without her knowledge:

NEW YORK, DEC. 26, 1881.

Charles Guiteau, Esq.:

Dear Sir: The expressed wish of a stranger that you have spent a "Merry," or a "Happy Christmas," would perhaps sound like a sarcasm. At the same time there are circumstances under which—

> "Stone walls do not a prison make,
> Nor iron bars a cage;
> Minds innocent and quiet take
> That for a hermitage"—

and I most sincerely hope you have been able to look upon your surroundings with complacency on this Christian anniversary.

In no heart did the assassination of President Garfield arouse more intense horror than in mine; yet there are few, if any, who can, today, sympathize with you more profoundly than I do.

This sympathy has its origin in a realization and appreciation, impossible to most persons, of the mysterious, subtle, and irresistible power of the delusion—as I must interpret your claim to "inspiration"—by which you were impelled, as I verily believe, to the dreadful deed, that will send the name of Garfield down to posterity as a martyr, and the name of Guiteau as a murderer, when, in fact and in truth, the one as little deserves the glory as the other the ignominy.

A Case of Insane Delusion.

I am only a woman, a Miss, and not very ancient; but I am certain there is no delusion so insidious, inciting, and propulsive as one arising from supposed inspiration. I speak from knowledge from having been the *confidante,* the close observer, and the custodian of a young lady whose "inspiration" nearly culminated in a sacrifice more unnatural and abhorrent than your attack upon the President.

This lady was, and is still, my dearest friend, an intimate from early childhood. Her father was a worthy and distinguished clergyman; her mother a devotee. She has three brothers and one sister, all of whom, excepting the younger brother, were noted, from their earliest adolescence for their exemplary conduct and Christian character. But no imputation or suspicion of fanaticism or bigotry was ever heard against any of the family, who, with their fervent piety, believed it to be the privilege and the duty of mankind to indulge their faculties and inclinations in every way, consistently with morality and religion, calculated to produce the greatest amount of enjoyment and happiness. In the lives of none were the principles and teachings of this creed more conspicuous than in the every-day conduct of my friend.

Her younger brother, as intimated a moment ago, is excepted from this complimentary description. Before he attained his majority he conceived a repugnance to Christian restraint and religious observances. He began by absenting himself from family prayers, smirking over grace at meals, inventing frivolous and false excuses for remaining from church, and in meeting the remonstrances and loving appeals of his parents with anger and defiance. Next, he fell into keeping late hours, and, as a little later discovered, bad company. In short, he went on *de mal en pis* until a *chronique scandaleuse* of his excesses and shortcomings would have included nearly all the sins and vices known to the Decalogue.

From the first the faults of her brother lay heavily at the heart of my friend. To her he was more than a brother; he seemed to her the better part of herself, for the two were twins. She loved, most fondly, the other members of the family, but this scapegrace she fairly idolized. It is but justice to him to say that he likewise adored her. Of this she was fully conscious, and it almost broke her heart because she could not reclaim him from his evil ways. His delinquencies and her solicitude for his future finally absorbed all her interest and thoughts. In her meditations and reflections, the mundane welfare of her brother found no place. His spiritual welfare and the danger to which he was exposing his soul, were her sole concern. In a word, she so pestered, pondered, prayed, and pined over his presumed peril that she became a monomaniac on that subject.

The condition of her intellect was discovered in this way: Her delusion, like that under which you labored, being a supposed inspiration from on high. One day she called at my home, and, after a brief chat in the parlor, requested to be conducted to my private room, saying she had an important communication to make in strict confidence. She appeared to be in the frame of mind that for some months had been usual with her, and, although I thought the request an odd one, as there was no one besides ourselves in the parlors, I readily acceded to it. As soon as she entered my room she went to the book-case, and, taking down the Bible, said, as she placed it on a table: "Put your hand on the Word of God and swear that you will never, without my permission, divulge the secret I am about to confide to you." There was in her face and carriage at this time an appearance of hopefulness and elation that I had not seen about her for several months; but this only served to make her demand the more startling. I told her I could not swear, as the Bible bids us "swear not at all." After considerable argument and persuasion she broke into a hearty laugh, and exclaimed:

"How absurd in me to ask you to swear—just as if I didn't know you would never betray a secret. Well, it is this," she went on after a moment's rejection, "can save W _____, my brother. God has promised to take him to His bosom and to pardon all his sins, and has commanded me to release him from the flesh, by the least painful means, as soon as possible."

I was astounded; almost stupefied. I knew that it was not possible for my friend to jest on so serious and sacred a subject, and besides I could see, under her sanguine, joyous air, that she was in dead earnest. Before I could recover sufficiently to express my astonishment she went on: "I must do it before Ash Wednesday, or he will worship Comus all through Lent, and then God might withdraw His promise to me. You see, I have only a fortnight to save him in, and I have no one but you to help me, you know."

"Help you! Great heaven, what are you talking about!" I fairly shrieked. In the most easy, businesslike way she proceeded: "Well, you see God, as well as my own heart, demands that I shall deliver him only through an euthanasia, and I don't know which of the many ways to choose. In a book of trials that we were once reading in your pa's study, there was something mentioned that released the soul from the body without any pain whatever; what was that?"

She alluded to a volume of Causes Celebres belonging to my father, a lawyer by profession, but for some years retired from practice. Then she told me of the various implements and instruments of death that had occurred to her as a means of "translating" (using the word in the sense you employ "removing") her brother from the temptations of Satan to the abode of bliss. Fearing she might act on her "inspiration" before proper steps could be devised to restrain her, or cure her malady, I pretended to humor her determination and scheme, and told her that I believed morphia would be the most merciful thing to use, as it would confer on her brother pleasant dreams, from which he would awake in the pleasanter realities of heaven.

She said she had thought of this, but that on applying to several druggists they had refused to sell her any. I told her that on the following day I should go to New York, and that I

182

would purchase a whole bottle full at a wholesale store. This pleased her, and she promised to wait.

When she was ready to return home I accompanied her, and made known her monomania to her parents. Several physicians were immediately consulted, and at the same time the author or cause of her derangement was informed of the mischief his deliquencies had wrought. His remorse was excruciating and terrible. After threatening to take his own life, in order that his sister's delusion might be brought to an end, he was asked, and eagerly consented, to cooperate with the physicians in a scheme which they believed would result in her cure.

This scheme, briefly stated, was as follows: I was to procure, or rather there was to be procured for me, a bottle of sulphate of morphia, and to assist her in preparing a sufficient quantity to produce the effect desired. After measuring and spreading out a sufficient quantity, I was, at a proper moment, to exchange it, without her knowledge, for an equal quantity of quinine.

Next, her brother, who frequently suffered from malaria, was to feign illness, and was to have quinine prescribed for him. Then I was to suggest, in case she failed to perceive it, that this would be an excellent opportunity for the execution of her project, since she could attend her brother and substitute morphine for quinine, and, as both were bitter, he would swallow the former without the least suspicion.

Further, the brother was to pretend, after taking the supposed narcotic, to fall into a profound slumber, and was to continue to appear in this state for at least two days. On "reviving" he was to pretend to have been in a trance—to have seen the angel of death, a panorama of his own sins, and also a glimpse of heaven and hell. He was to supplement this with the announcement that, having seen the folly and wickedness of the erratic life he had been leading, he was determined to reform and devote the remainder of his days to honorable, noble, and Christian pursuits.

The whole programme, of which I have given you only a vague epitome, was successfully carried out. The "trance" continued upwards of three days, and though my friend repeatedly saw her brother, and believed him on the verge of dissolution, she never once betrayed the least compunction. When her brother "awoke" and described his "visions," which were as picturesque as Dante's Visions of Hell, Purgatory, and Paradise, and expressed contrition—as pathetic as the confessions of Rousseau—at the sinful and scandalous course be had followed, the sister listened with a wistful, disappointed air, and evidently regretted that her purpose bad miscarried. But when, later on, be proceeded to explain that he had also experienced a change of heart, and that thenceforth he was determined to lead a Christian and useful life, she threw herself on his neck and, weeping for joy, frantically thanked God that her brother's life as well as his soul had been spared. Her "inspiration," her delusion, ended with the cause that produced it. She frankly stated to her family her intention, and attempt to remove her brother from vices and sins that threatened to destroy his soul. At the same time she was told how her scheme had been circumvented.

My Case.

I have given this narrative, Mr. Guiteau, because the case of my friend bears, in numerous ways, a striking resemblance to your own, and because I have indulged the hope that it may be some gratification to you to learn that, notwithstanding the clamor of the newspapers, there are people in the world who, whilst they regret Mr. Garfield's violent taking off, can understand the character of the impulse that forced you to the commission of the deed, and see in you something better than a murderer. There are a greater number of people of this kind than the men, who, for lucre and fame are clamoring for your blood, appear to think. As a matter of interest, my friend, who under a delusion similar to that affecting you, came so near to committing fratricide, and myself, resolved a few days ago to call on one hundred lady friends and get their opinions as to whether you were at the time of shooting Garfield responsible to God or man for the act. Our calls were made promiscuously on the wives and daughters of lawyers, doctors, clergymen, bankers, merchants, and other respectable laymen, and out of the one hundred opinions—only one lady in each family being called on to express one—there were but seven who believed you to have been actuated by a malignant and murderous spirit, and one of these was an intimate friend of Mr. Garfield, and another was too ignorant to know the difference between a sane and insane delusion.

From this test it is obvious that if you were to be tried before a jury composed of ladies you would be promptly acquitted; and yet, previous to the commencement of your trial, my sex in this section were unanimously convinced of your guilt, and would have voted, if called upon, that the extreme penalty should be inflicted upon you. I can also assure you that since your trial began there has also been a great change among members of your own sex in their views as to your moral and legal accountability; but the change is not so great by perhaps twenty- five per cent, as among mothers and daughters.

Ingratitude of the Stalwarts.

But there is one point in which you have concern, in which a vast majority of my male acquaintances agree with the unanimous opinion of women, and that is, that the treatment, the neglect, you have suffered at the hands of President Arthur and other Stalwart Republicans, who owe their elevation to you, is simply infamous! There is a proverb that Republics are ungrateful, but henceforth it should be specially applied to Republicans of the Arthur-Conkling-Cameron stripe.

> "If there be a crime
> Of deeper die than all the guilty train
> Of human vices, 'tis ingratitude"—

the poet has well and truly said, so truly that a later poet has more briefly put it—

> "Ingratitude is treason to mankind."

The political history of the world may be searched in vain for an example or instance of ingratitude so base, black, and brutal as that of the men you have elevated to power and fortune. Whether you were sane or insane when you fired the fatal shot they were bound to gain, and you to lose; and, sane or insane, you have claim upon their moral and material support. The pretended sympathy, the crocodile tears, some of them shed over Garfield, need not prevent their seeing even-handed justice done by you. If they lack the courage to aid you openly they should have done it stealthily. They should, at the very least, have provided you with counsel, whose ability and experience would enable them to cope with prosecuting array. A legal gentleman told me a few evenings ago that he knew, as a fact, that a single intimation by word or look from President Arthur would (some time ago when the trial was being talked over by a number of friends in New York) have secured you the services of John Graham, the greatest lawyer in criminal practice living at this time. He was one of the leading counsel for Sickles, was counsel-in-chief for McFarland, and for scores of other defendants in criminal cases, and his record of successes eclipse that of any other American advocate. The gentleman I mentioned and my father, also a lawyer, are of opinion that Mr. Graham would have been able to acquit you, and (for him) quite easily.

I am sure you will, in consideration of my sex, and my solicitude for your future, and in consideration of my assurance that there are thousands upon thousands who sympathize and pray for your speedy deliverance, favor me with at least so much of an acknowledgment of the receipt of this as will ensure me your autograph. If you will enclose half a dozen more, that I may distribute among your most ardent friends, they will be immensely esteemed. And now, *au revoir.* May God protect and deliver you, is the sincere prayer of your stranger friend.

SUNDAY EVENING, JAN. 1, 1882.

Mr. Guiteau:

From the bottom of my heart I am wishing you "A Happy New Year." Most sincerely do I wish that you could be one of the many who will call upon me tomorrow. I mean that I wish you were free to call on everybody, wherever inclination might lead you. Doubtless you will receive, yourself, calls enough; for there is not, I presume, living a human being, not excepting Vic-

186

toria the virtuous, or Alexander the autocrat, whom the people of every class would take so much interest in seeing, as yourself; but many of these, I fear, will have as little sympathy with you as the masses are said to have had with the great king remover, or "king maker," of four centuries ago, the Earl of Warwick, Still he, like yourself, had his friends, and posterity appreciates, if it does not applaud his conduct.

I penned my letter of Christmas without consulting anybody, but when I showed it to my mother she objected to my sending it without leave of my father, who was absent on business in St. Louis, and was not expected home until the end of the year. He returned yesterday, and although he did not quite approve of my writing you, he at length, to get rid of my importunity I suppose, gave me permission to send my letter.

He also gave me permission to report some things he said last evening, in conversation with our family physician, who had made a neighborly call. He says he thinks your counsel could have educed, on the cross-examination of the Government experts, certain admissions which would go far towards sustaining the theory of the defense. He thinks these witnesses, if still at the capital, should be called back to the stand for further cross-examination, which, he says the court would permit as matter of favor, if not of right. Should it refuse, he says, he would, if he were counsel, call these witnesses to the stand at the risk of making them witnesses as to the matters to be inquired into for the defense.

Views of a Lawyer.

Father claims, if I understand his views, which I cannot persuade him to indite, or even dictate to me, though he has twice orally repeated them, that the prosecution has through a myopism that nothing but passion could produce, stultified itself in a vital matter. He declares that in their obvious endeavor to give you, Mr. Guiteau, a character, and fasten on you a disposition and propensities in keeping with, and calculated to suggest and prompt the motive and considerations that they claim induced you to shoot Garfield have adduced a mass of evidence intended to present you to the jury as the incarnation of vanity, egotism, and ambition; and that if half this evidence is true it is overwhelmingly conclusive, unfortunate for the prosecution, that you have been a monomaniac, or more still, a duomaniac for years. This evidence of the prosecution, he claims, is more than sufficient to prove that you have, for a long time, been the victim of two distinct species or varieties of monomania. One he calls the monomania of pride and ambition; that is, a malady born of the exaltation of self-esteem and egotism; the other a monomania of vanity; an unnatural, irrational craving for applause, notoriety or grandeur. He mentioned other names (of technical character, I suppose) for these monomanics, but for my life, though I tried to fix them in my mind, I cannot recall them, nor can it matter.

Perhaps I ought to explain that pa did not mean to say, and that I do not believe, you have the mental derangements mentioned, but only that, assuming the State's evidence to be true, you must have been, as he expresses it, *non compos mentis* for at least a decade; and he thinks the prosecutors deserve for their malignant, unconscionable blind rage, to be hoist with their own petard, or floored with their own heathenish boomerang.

These monomanies, pa says, are recognized by the best authorities as well defined species of insanity, and that, considering the political situation at the time, the tendencies of these maladies, or either of them, might well have precipitated their victim on the President, under the delusion that he would win the world's applause, or realize his ambitious aspirations.

Although pa believes you might—thanks to the testimony for the people—have been successfully defended under these varieties of insanity, it is not with this view that he suggests that your counsel should further cross-examine the experts.

He would merely have them admit before the jury that the best authorities on insanity recognize a monomania of vanity and self-esteem; and, as a distinct variety of insanity, a monomania of pride and ambition. Then he would have them asked whether a person afflicted with both, or either, of these maladies would not be more susceptible to an insane delusion—a supposed divine inspiration—than one who had betrayed no

188

symptoms of insanity, and who was perfectly sane until the manifestation of such delusion.

Next, whether an inspiration or delusion, such as it is claimed impelled you to the shooting, would not be more likely to enter into and control a victim to the monomanies specified than to take possession of a person hitherto in good mental health.

I cannot get the questions in the phraseology pa used, but I think I caught his ideas, and your lawyers can do the rest if the suggestions are worth anything.

He also said he would call; no, I am not sure, but that he said he would venture to ask the Government experts still further whether one afflicted with the monomanies indicated would not (your circumstances and surroundings all considered) be more likely to become a victim of the delusion that led to the shooting, than would one affected by the monomania of fear, of kleptomania, or dipsomania.

And now. Mr. Guiteau, I am done. I have written you, not that I sympathize in your deed, but because I believe you, honestly believed, that you were doing God's bidding, and if the worst must come that you will feel and be able to say with Charlotte Corday when she killed Murat, *"C'estle crime qui fait la honte, et non pas Vechafaud."* But if my prayers will avail, a better fate is in reserve for you. God's will will be done.

(Postscript).

Mr. Guiteau:

I was pleased to read in the *Herald* this morning that on Sunday and yesterday you received quite an ovation from the people of Washington. If you did not have "A Happy New Year," you certainly could have had little time to brood over your unfortunate situation, or to feel miserable.

But I was pained to see in the same paper a report that you are to be deprived of the few comforts you have been, of late, permitted to enjoy; namely, your mail and palatable meals. I can hardly believe this report. To deprive you of the first would be an outrage upon your personal rights; to deny you the second would be a piece of cruelty that would bring discredit and reproach on all responsible for the deprivation or neglect.

Knowing how busy you must be at the present time, I enclose an envelope already superscribed and stamped, in which you can, with little loss of time, enclose your autograph, or still better, such reply as your feelings may dictate.

Father goes to Washington Friday evening. I have extorted a promise that I may accompany him and that he will take me to court; but he refuses to take me to the jail. Unless I can coax him before his departure to do this, or let some friends take me to the jail, I shall pout and be disagreeable and stay at home. I would, I know, be very glad to go to the capital with him for a few weeks' visit, as we have many friends there; but I will not go unless I can be free to have my own way. Whether I go or stay, I shall hope to receive, at least, a word, though I hope for several, at your first convenience.

And now once more, *au revoire*—for I hate the words "farewell." and "adieu," and "good bye," as I do death.

NEW YORK, WEDNESDAY EVENING, JAN. 11, 1882.
Charles Guiteau, Esq.:

My Dear Sir: Your letter of the 7th inst. came promptly to hand. It is needless to assure you, after what I said in my former letter, that it is highly appreciated. It will be esteemed and preserved as long as I live, and I doubt not, for many generations when we are no more, as a most interesting and solemn *souvenir* of the most important drama in the history of the Republic, and of yourself, the principal actor, and now central figure. I do not prize it, as a gentleman acquaintance was rude enough last evening to intimate, as a memento of the political annihilation of President Garfield, for although I had freely indulged my right, (as most young ladies in my social circle do, in accordance with their predilections or prejudices) to criticize and condemn some of the acts of Mr. Garfield, I can asseverate, from the inmost recess of my heart, that no one unconnected with him by consanguineal or hymeneal ties, could have felt more sincere and profound sorrow than I did at his death. I prize it because I believe, or rather know, that you will either be acquitted and come forth a free man, whose claims upon his party and country will then be recognized, or you will fall a victim to an unjust administration of the law, and take an honored place in glory beside St. Paul and a host of lesser martyrs; and in either case I shall prize your letter as the most precious *souvenir* that I could possess.

The four autographs you were kind enough to enclose were all begged away by lady friends, who, like myself, sympathize deeply with you. Although I had intended to preserve one for my album I could not, in face of my good fortune in having your letter, be so selfish.

I had hoped to see you, and I still indulge the hope of meeting you at no remote day, but pa, who, dear soul, is the most indulgent of parents, felt constrained to refuse my petition to visit you at the jail. He desired that I should accompany him to Washington where he now is, and promised to take me to the court that I might see you, but I declined the offer. I wished to speak to you as well as to see you. Moreover, I knew it would cost me more patience and pain than I could well endure to sit quietly and hear those cold-blooded men clamor for your immolation. Pa would sacrifice much of his own feelings, not involving what he regards the proprieties of society, to gratify me; but we are so well known in Washington that he thinks it would be next to impossible for me to call, even with himself and friends, at the jail to see you, without provoking unpleasant criticism and notoriety; especially as he, although not a politician, strictly speaking, is a very pronounced Stalwart. But I know from his remarks that should you, unfortunately be convicted, he will see less objection to my visiting you with friends before you should be granted a new trial. In such case, he says, there would be far less danger of our motives being misunderstood and misrepresented; that the act, which might now be interpreted as an approval of Garfield's taking-off, would then be ascribed to Christian charity. Pa, I have no doubt is right, but, at the same time, I think with the Sartor Resartus that our true inwardness and best motives, as well as the worst, are hidden too much "in clothes."

Then should you (which God forbid) be condemned I shall see you; and if you are vindicated and set free I hope to see you, though in the latter contingency the realization of my wish

191

will depend upon yourself. You request me to send you my photograph, and I shall do so, although I have with great difficulty succeeded in obtaining mamma's consent. Pa had left for Washington before your letter arrived, and ma has feared that some of the keepers might find the photograph and give it to some of the enterprising artists of the illustrated papers, who would give it publicity. But I have at length succeeded in convincing her that you will not, especially after having your attention drawn to the danger, allow such an accident to happen. I will endeavor to send one with this epistle, but if I do not I will send one in a day or two. On looking around the house I have not able to find one of dimensions that will accommodate themselves to a letter; that is, none recently taken, though I have several of larger size, 8 by 12 inches, but I think I may get one from some of my friends, near by, who have complimented me by pilfering my image—not for its beauty —but for—I don't know what. (After that punctuation I ought to have added, "I'll be *dashed* (—) if I do.") But it makes me so fidgety when I think of your situation, of which I had a partial illustration in the mania of my friend, that I can scarcely write intelligibly much less look to the rules of prosody. But, as I was saying, if I do not, after closing my letter, find a photo among my near friends, I will go over to the city and get some taken, and send one tomorrow or the next day.

You will not imagine, I am sure, that I could misconceive your wish and request to have my picture. I can easily understand that in your confined and isolated situation you would, or might, derive some little solace and comfort from glancing over the miniatures—since you cannot have present the originals—of those who sympathize and are praying for your deliverance.

I suppose it would be useless to ask for a photograph of yourself, as you are situated. I have all the illustrated papers that gave a picture of you, and had in my mind's eye formed a satisfactory likeness of you; but father, who saw you in court, in a letter received yesterday, declares that none of these pictures closely resemble you, and that most of them are caricatures. He adds, however, that the tonsorial operation performed on you previous to the taking a cast of your head must have made some change in your facial appearance, yet that he is assured by Judge Porter that the pictures never gave a striking or faithful representation of you.

You must have seen pa. as his conversation with Porter was in court. They are old friends, and pa says he is confident that if Porter—though he has many superiors— had defended, he could have brought you out in triumph. His *forte* is well understood to lie rather in defending than in prosecuting.

I am glad you are to make the closing speech in your defense, and I hope and believe the effort will be worthy of the occasion and of yourself. As Porter is to follow you in closing for the prosecution, I pray that, apart from the merits, you will do and say everything possible to neutralize, in advance, the effect of his euphonistic declamation and rhetoric. If you will bear in mind that I am a lawyer's daughter, and one who has always, for years at least, taken a great interest in legal controversies and forensic warfare, (often wishing myself a man), you will, I am certain, take in good part the suggestions I may make for combatting Porter and Davidge.

Porter and Davidge.

I do not think you could give Porter a harder blow than by likening him and his grandiloquent periods to Sergeant Buzfuz, in the great case of Mrs. Bardell *versus* Pickwick. You doubtless remember how that great disciple of Themis undertook to prove a breach of promise from Pickwick's notes, the first of which, pertaining to a dinner to be provided, was as follows: "Garrawa's, twelve o'clock. Dear Mrs. B _____: Chops and tomato sauce. Yours, Pickwick." Buzfuz, you know, endeavored to make this note—the viand and vegetable mentioned being claimed to be terms of endearment—with other like evidence, prove the courtship, breach of promise, and all If you do not remember the case well and clearly borrow Pickwick Papers, and you will soon see how you can hit Porter severely, and at the same time recommend yourself to the jury and the country. No more telling illustration of Porter's style and pretensions here could be given.

Another good hit you can give Porter is this: He lays claim to excellence, not only as a lawyer, but as a *literatus*—a *dilettante,* or rather a *cognoscente.* Arraign Porter for his assurance, his egotism, fluency, and euphonism, and then quote from the *Spectator,* No. 484, against him. The article shows how men with conceit rise to eminence by wordy noise, where men of talent, with modesty, remain below; and you have only to give this quotation from the *Spectator* to cut him deeply.

"I must confess when I have seen Charles Frankair rise up with a commanding mien, and torrent of handsome words, talk a mile off the purpose, and drive down boobies of ten times his sense, who at the same time were envying his impudence and despising his understanding, it has been matter of great mirth to me."

This I take it would be a nut-shell view of the interior of the court-room. You can make a good point of this with the jury if you take time to elaborate it. Get the book if you can, though my introduction is accurate and the quotation *verbatim.*

And now, a word about Mr. Davidge. Pa laughed a good deal about Mr. Davidge's employment by the Government now, when only a few years ago be appeared in court against the Government; not as counsel, but as a witness—an *expert* witness. He was called as a legal expert, and expert as to the law of the United States relating to treason, in the proceedings at Montreal for the extradition of the St. Albans raiders. Mr. Davidge was called to prove that the acts of *robbery* and *murder* committed by this predatory gang at St. Albans would constitute treason under the laws and Constitution of the United States. Mr. "Expert" Davidge, pa (who was present on the occasion) says, swore it all, without blushing. It was his testimony, mainly, upon which the robbers and murderers were discharged.

Now, I think from my observation of the trial—your trial—as it has been presented by the newspapers, that Mr. Davidge will be the counsel appointed to have most to say about "experts." You will therefore have an opportunity to set him out nicely, and I believe yours is one of that numerous class of cases in which it is only necessary to knock down (figuratively, of course) the prosecuting attorneys to destroy their cause. You may, then, on the "expert" line, hang up Mr. Davidge like a green goose, and make him feel that "the goose hangs high" on the wrong side of the mouth. O, I would I were a man; how I would like to get my tongue on that pretentious, inflated old Copperhead!

I had thought only to give you a manuscript copy of Davidge's testimony referred to, but, Mr. Guiteau, to prevent the old rebel from disputing you, I shall cut a leaf containing his testimony from the printed report of the St. Albans case. The book is a large one, and at this time it would, I suppose, be impossible to purchase a copy at any price, in any store in Canada or the United States. Pa, I know, thinks it contains the best and most exhaustive arguments on various points of international law that have ever been delivered and published. You can, therefore, understand how much above money's worth he values this book which contains every word of the testimony and a word-for-word copy of the arguments of the distinguished counsel.

Now I shall venture without father's leave—as he is still in Washington—to cut out the leaf containing Davidge's testimony and send it to you that you may confront him should he—good Government man as he now is—attempt to dispute your arraignment of his record as a patriot, a citizen, and an expert. Perhaps it would be better in "pitching into him," to have the leaf, the proof of his Copperheadism or disloyalty, at hand, and shake it in his face at the first moment of arraigning him. This if dramatically done would confound him and extort from his face and manner a confession of guilt. Davidge's testimony, as legal expert, was short, (it was on a *hypothetical* question, too), because the counsel for the U.S. refused, as they did as to most witnesses, to cross-examine. But it should be remembered that Mr. Davidge was the *only* "expert" on the law that was called. He did all that was required on that branch of the case; and you can, if you assail him heartily, drive him in shame from the court.

You will, I am sure, remembering how I have taken the responsibility to cut out this leaf, take good care to preserve and

195

return it to me. I have removed it with care so that I can replace it without leaving any sign of mutilation visible. I should have sent the book entire, but that I am inclined to think it would never reach you or return to me. Mr. Davidge, I know, would take pleasure in giving it over to the devouring element. Then as soon as you have made use of the extract, please enclose it to me for replacement.

I pray to heaven that you will not spare these men. Show the inconsistency of Davidge's attitude as an expert eighteen years ago against his Government, and now, in a *spirit of repentance,* raking up experts for the purposes of a Government prosecution. This, with a bit of good mimicry, with Buzfuz as an illustration, which will disarm the polished rhetoric of Porter in a great degree, will, I do believe, have more effect on the chances of the trial than all the evidence introduced; all the logic, solid reasoning, and law that the case has called forth. Frequent ejaculations during Porter's speech of "Chops and tomato sauce,"—or, as Buzfuz in one place exclaims to the jury, "Chops! Gracious heavens! and tomato sauce!"—would bring down the house and destroy the effect of Porter's magniloquent periods.

You could make your comparison of Porter to Buzfuz the more neat and effective if you had the Pickwick Papers to refer to and read from in making your illustration. At any rate, you ought to have the book in jail to glance over the Buzfuz argument, and I would mail it to you but that I am assured it would never be permitted to reach you. So, borrow a copy, or, as brother tells me that it was published in the Seaside Series, under the title of *Pickwick Papers*, you could make your brother get it for you. The Buzfuz argument, &c. will be found in chapter 34. By means of this case, Pa once so ridiculed an argument of Mr. O'Conor, which he could not have met with the logic of facts or the law, that he achieved an unexpected and undeserved victory. It will stand you in equally good stead.

THURSDAY, JAN. 12, 1882.

Mr. Guiteau:

I abstained from closing my letter last evening, thinking I

might wish to add something today. I observed in this morning's *Herald*, that you had a call yesterday from a photographer, and that you will set to him after you have made your closing speech. Perhaps, then, it will be possible for me, after all, to get a faithful likeness of you. It may not be convenient for you to send me one—though it would be the more prized if received from your own hand—but if you will inform me of the name and address of the artist, or how I can obtain the picture, I will send for one before they are all gone. If I do not send you mine with this letter, I will enclose it tomorrow or next day. I am going over to New York as soon as I close, and on my way shall drive around to two or three friends who may have small pictures of me.

And now, Mr. Guiteau, I must say *au revoir.* I am compelled to conclude rather abruptly, as I had coaxed brother, who is attending Columbia College, to wait and take the carriage with me, just as he was about to take a car; and he has just sent up word to hurry me. I pray
God may give you strength, wisdom, and skill to make a successful defense. May He inspire you with the grandest and loftiest ideas and fancies, and give you a preternatural command of the most solemn and sublime words in our language, with which to impress on the jury your irresponsibility and guiltlessness—to make them feel that—

> Truth crush'd to earth, shall never rise again;
> The eternal years of God are hers,"

and that it will be better for their peace of mind and for their future, if they uphold it now, rather than have it rise before them hereafter; that if they crush it to earth now it will be recorded against them and crush them when they are judged by a court that cannot err. And, oh! may you soon be restored to liberty, to the world, where you will find more numerous and appreciative friends than you have ever before known.
Prayerfully yours,

NEW YORK, FRIDAY EVENING, JAN. 20, 1882.
Mr. Guiteau:

My Dear Persecuted Friend: When I closed my latest letter to you I expected ere this to have sent you, as a token of sympathy and of confidence in your honor, my photograph. With that letter in hand I left home intending—with a view of complying with your request the sooner—if possible to procure one of my pictures from a near friend, and in case of failure, to immediately have some new copies taken. After sealing and mailing my letter, I dropped brother up town and drove at once to the home of a lady cousin in Twenty-third street, whom I had thought to make accompany me to a photographer's. She is one of the very few friends I have to whom I could willingly explain the reason of my being so pressed for a picture as to seek it in such disagreeable weather; and reaching the house I found her ill—sick enough to be in bed—although she had retired the night before in the best of spirits, and apparently in excellent health.

Of course I could not ask my poor cousin to accompany *me;* but she did ask me to remain with her, which I should have done unasked; and there I have been ever since until noon today, when I left my patient rapidly convalescing. Tomorrow, unless the state of the weather forbids, I will either find or sit for a photograph. If prevented tomorrow, I will take advantage of the next available day. You shall not, my friend, be disappointed, though I cannot flatter myself that your disappointment would be as intense as mine would be at not receiving a picture of you.

Your last two letters post-marked respectively the 13th and 17th insts. (which for some inexplicable cause were delivered simultaneously), were delivered to me by brother yesterday morning. I would have replied at once, but I could not compose my mind sufficiently to do so. Pleased, thankful, as I was to receive your letters. I cannot, even yet, tell whether they gave me more pleasure, or pain. As I read the latest, penned in jail, giving expression to the noble sentiments, aspirations, and hopes animating your bosom, my heart swelled with sympathetic rapture; when I arrived at the end of the paragraph, when I came to your observations on the realities of your situation, I seemingly felt, as a cold perspiration burst from my forehead, the frigid touch of prison walls, and heard the clanging of bolts and chains.

O, my poor friend, how can you in such surroundings, so implicitly indulge anticipations of justice! I own that this faith, this sublime faith, in one sense pleases me. To my mind it is irrefragable evidence that you sincerely believe in your claim of inspiration. But, my dear friend, is it
wise that you should so confidently look forward to life and liberty? God knows I would not have you give way to disappointment and despair; would not have you cower or cry—

> "Mine after-life! what is mine after-life?
> My day is closed! the gloom of night is come!
> A hopeless darkness settles o'er my fate!"

No; I would have you hold no commerce with despair. I would have you hope and draw from that celestial passion all the comfort and strength that the consciousness of innocence will reasonably justify one, persecuted by popular malice and the utmost power of governing politicians. I would have you hope, but would have you at the same time remember, that "hope is fortune's cheating lottery," where for one prize there are a hundred blanks. I would have you remember that you are being tried (most unfairly tried) under human (not divine) law, and would have you not forget that a host of men and woman, inspired of God, have, in His inscrutable wisdom, been allowed, whilst devoting their best energies to His service, to perish by the most cruel and ignominious contrivances that human ingenuity could invent. I would have you, whilst never doubting the genuineness of your inspiration to remove Garfield, bear in mind that it may have been a part of the divine dispensation that your own mortal part should build still higher the hecatomb of martyrs that has been reared by that Christian Moloch, that profane trinity, passion, prejudice, and perversive power.

> "The ways of heaven are dark and intricate;
> Puzzled with mazes and perplexed with error,
> Our understanding searches them in vain."

We only know that God moves in a mysterious way His wonders to perform. And I would have you, dear friend, prepared to smile with complacency on any freak of fickler fortune; to meet with courage and fortitude the worst possibility that can lie in the future; to face death, if condemned by the court and jury, like a martyr, without faltering, flinching, or fear. I would have you, whilst feeling that human justice had been denied you, believe that, like Peter, Paul, and many others, you are as an instrument of God on earth, left to suffer in fulfilment of a preordained destiny. I would have realize now, that—

> "Alas! there is no stay in human state,
> No one can shun inevitable fate;
> The doom was written, the decree was past,
> Ere the foundations of the world were cast."

No; I would not have you; it would be too terrible.

Sunday Evening, 9.25 o'clock.

At the above point I was interrupted by a call from a gentleman acquaintance. I had twice within a half hour been "not at home" to callers, but the third call was from a gentleman who is to sail by the Parthia on Wednesday, to finish his university career at Heidelberg, and I could not refuse to say *au revoir;* the more especially as he once saved my life at the risk of his own. It was too late to resume my letter when he departed and yesterday, O! what a miserable Saturday it was. I had the *ennui* from morning till night. I couldn't have touched a pen, pencil, brush, book, or needle, to have won a new compliment. After reading the conclusion of Mr. Scoville's argument I challenged brother, who, on account of the weather had remained at home, to contend at chess; then at billiards, and finally at target-shooting with both bow and pistol; and though I was defeated in all these for the first time by this adversary, it failed to set my sluggish blood in circulation and throw off the depression. It would have looked absurd, and would have been cruelty to horses to have driven around in quest of one of my pictures, and would have been an unfit day to sit for one. This last was the reason I did not attempt to finish my letter. I thought that as I must wait for the photo, I would wait to finish writing. So, after failing to get clear of the blues, I unconditionally surrendered myself to laziness and languor, and drooped and moped—now playing a selection from Rienzi backwards, and singing the Marseillaise to the air of Yankee Doodle; now spinning around on the piano-stool and imagining myself a top; then, with my nose flattened against the window-pane, watching the rain, the boats plying the river, and the elevated trains (or the long lines of smoke from them) as they bowled like ten-pin balls, along the streets of New York. Finally, when almost sun-set, I clipped a few flowers for the dinner-table, thinking the while how I would like to make up a bouquet, which should, in the language of flowers, express some of my thoughts and feelings, to place on your table, or in the window beside the potted plants provided by the tender hands and thoughtful care of your sister. Little did I think—nor would any one be likely to suppose—that this thought or wish would lead me to the commission of a criminal act; nevertheless such was the case. When dinner was half over, brother, whom I had noticed from time to time eyeing me critically, suddenly exclaimed Good heavens. Gus, are you out of your head?" "No, but I think you must be," I replied; "what in the world are you staring at me in that absurd way for?" I very soon learned the "why" and the "wherefore." It was all on account of a camelia that I wore in my bosom, and which, Eve-like, I had plucked from a forbidden tree or shrub.

Last autumn when we returned from abroad, brother, who from a child has shown a passion for flowers and floriculture, almost amounting to a mania, brought home with him, besides a box of cuttings and layings, a potted camelia—the gift of one of the greatest florists in France— the result of fifteen year's hybridization of camelia *japonica, reticulata*, and the *oleifera*, in all their varieties, the like of which has never yet been seen in any private conservatory in Europe, still less in this country. Well, a few days ago this priceless plant put forth a bud which, unfolding itself, threw brother into estacies. It was a fine flower, truly, as all camelias are, but, to my notion, was not the bell of the conservatory. In making up a dinner vase I had, with other exotics, clipped quite a number of Camelias of various sorts, and I do not think anything led me to pluck the new foreigner for my bosom but the circumstance of its standing alone. All camelias, in the language of flowers, alike mean "pity," you know, and it must have been its forlorn condition; its emblematic character, coinciding with the thoughts and sympathy excited by your solitary and desolate situation, which had been uppermost in my mind all day, that impelled me, mechanically, to commit the awful crime. But didn't I catch it? Such a scolding! I offered to tie or glue the flower back on the plant, but even that did not appease brother's wrath. After getting nearly out of breath he wound up, "By gracious, it is worse than Guiteau pulling up turnips for weeds. I tell you, mother, that ever since you let Gus correspond with that lunatic she has been as crazy as he is"—quite a compliment to you as well as to myself. But when I said demurely, "I hope you will forgive me, Livy, for I do assure you the poor flower appeared so isolated and lonely that I heard it, as I passed, exclaim 'pity,' and in pity I took it to my bosom;" as I said this he fell to laughing, and I really believe he forgave me.

I have told all this about myself, Mr. Guiteau, that you may see what a foolish, cranky sort of person your correspondent is. And having done this I shall put my letter aside until Monday afternoon or evening, when I shall know whether I can send you a photograph without having, in this disagreeable weather, to go and sit for one. Though the picture will hardly repay the interest you take in it, you shall surely have it.

Monday Evening, P. M.

Mr. Guiteau:

"When on Friday evening I was interrupted, I was speaking in regard to your confident expectation of an acquittal. I do not know precisely what more I would have said, had I been left undisturbed, but my principal purpose was to caution you against permitting your consciousness of innocence, your natural desire, and sanguine temperament to elevate your faith and anticipations to such a height that disappointment would prove, if not insupportable, too intense for dignified concealment. "Blessed are they that expect nothing," says the divine word, "for they shall not be disappointed." I would not have you indulge in

"Those high-built hopes that crush us by their fall."

I would not have you die from excessive joy on the one hand, or from disappointment on the other. A conviction would be hard enough to bear, even if you are well prepared for it. It would be a thousand times harder to bear if you are overconfidently expecting an acquittal. O, if a thought or suggestion from me should, in case you are condemned, serve to mitigate the immediate force of the terrible blow, how thankful I should be!

But I have in mind not only your feelings but your fame, your character for courage. If the foreman of that jury pronounces the word "guilty," I would have you prepared to swallow the verdict as the ancient boxer, whose incisors had been knocked from the sockets by his adversary, swallowed his teeth with a smile and with a composure that shall disappoint the rabble and vindictive, who hope to be regaled with reports of your trepidation and agony. It is certain that your doom will not be decided by this trial even should the verdict be against you, and a modest exhibition of fortitude and mild defiance will go far to aid you in public opinion and otherwise in the future.

"The truly brave,
When they behold the brave assail'd by odds,
Are touched with a desire to shield or save."

And if, finally, the law fails to do you justice—or I should say if the instruments of the law, judges and jurors, fail to try you impartially and deal out equity—or, in other words, if the persistent clamor of the press (and with a blush be it said, of the pulpit) and the consequent howls of the hollow-headed masses, are to override law and justice—if you are to be pushed, persecuted, and pursued to death, like a mad bull in the Plaza de Toros, may your courage and fortitude be such that the picadores, chulos, matador, and spectators—that is to say, the counsel, court, executioner, and public shall be compelled to declare, with Childe Harold's description of the brave bull in the arena—

"Slowly he falls, amidst triumphing cries,
Without a groan, without a struggle, dies."

Bennett, of the "Herald."

There are many who predict that in the event of your final condemnation and execution, you will break down and die a craven and dastard. This is a vaticination of that miserable *Herald*, whose owner's pusillanimity and cowardice has made him a notorious laughing-stock both in this country and Europe. I have more than once seen in drawing-rooms in London and Paris sly winks and contemptuous smiles, and heard derisive remarks, not a yard from his elbow, concerning the horse-whipping he received and avenged with blank cartridges. I would have the prediction false, if only to disappoint that wretched poltroon. I would have him and others like him condemned, like those damned souls of Dante, who, for their predictions, had their faces turned behind, and were compelled for all eternity to walk backwards. No one but a beastly coward at heart, though believing you guilty, would anticipate and comment with satisfaction on the probability, born of his wishes, that you would meet an ignominious and inhuman death, with manifestations of agony, despair, weakness, and fear.

I cannot believe, my friend, that such a fate is in store for you. I cannot believe that any honest jury would convict you in the absence of any adequate personal motive for the deed. But still I beg you to be not too confident of an acquittal, but to be fully prepared to accept with stoicism and nonchalance any verdict that may come. Should you be convicted many good lawyers are of opinion that you will receive a new trial, and in that case I promise you that you shall not be convicted again. I, with other ladies of my acquaintance, have vowed to find you counsel able to cope with and vanquish Mr. Porter and his associates.

Tuesday Evening, 8 o'clock.
My Dear Poor Friend:

You seemed to have received the impression that Pa's refusal to let me visit you at the jail was prompted by pride or loftiness, or repugnance or aversion. This is not by any means the case. Pa, although not a politician, is a Stalwart of the first water, and he feared that the circumstance of his visiting you in jail, or of permitting me to do so, would, should it become known, be interpreted as an approval of your course. This consideration has without doubt kept hundreds of persons who sympathize with you from calling at the jail. But, for my part, I do not at all believe in this caution or circumspection. It smacks of timidity and hypocrisy.

Ingratitude of the Stalwarts.

So far as Stalwart politicians who have been benefited by Garfield's death are concerned, I think their conduct has been in the last degree heartless and infamous. Arthur, Conkling, Grant, and others were glad, were delighted, when the news of Garfield's fall was flashed over the wires. When it was believed he would recover they prayed that he might die. When death came they pretended to grieve, whilst their hearts were overflowing with exultation; and by his bier wept crocodile tears. There is not one of them who does not believe that the Republican Party has been saved and the country benefited by your act. And yet not one of them has had the heart or manliness to do one thing to save you from the gallows, or ensure you evenhanded justice. I would not, of course, expect them to fly openly to your assistance, but they could have aided you, and if they had a grain of gratitude in their souls they would have done so stealthily. But on the contrary, they have all of them, Senator Logan excepted, been helping to immolate you. Should you be convicted and sentenced I am certain that President Arthur, who owes his elevation entirely to you, would allow you to be hanged like a dog. O, Mr. Guiteau, I implore you that in case the worst should come, as I imagine such a climax, in spite of all endeavor to drive it from my thoughts. Sometimes I see you resisting your executioners, fighting with the desperation of despair for your life. At others, I see you walk to the fatal trap with manly dignity and composure, and submit your head to the murderous rope. O, horror of horrors! I feel at such times that I must fly to you to save you. I can hardly suppress my shrieks, while I tremble and shudder like an aspen, as tears and cold sweat pour from me like rain.

But I cannot and will not believe that the court will be so deaf to the appeals of justice and mercy as to consign you, in defiance of law, human and divine, to so terrible an end. God has said "A tree shall be judged by its fruit." Your tree, the tree that Porter and his associates are denouncing, brought forth fruit that reunited and saved from dissolution the Republican Party, and saved the country as well, and for this you are, they insist, to be hewn down; I do not and will not believe it. And when, within five minutes I shall close my letter, I shall fall on my knees and pray, as I have for weeks done every night, that God may spare your life and restore you to liberty.

And now, my poor friend, good-night. I have written you a long letter; but have not said one of the many things I would, if circumstances permitted, most like to say. I trust, indeed—"I feel it in my bones," to use a common expression of brother's—that we shall some time meet, and meet outside of prison walls. Good-night, and may the just and merciful God protect and bless you.

Thursday Morning,

(The day after my conviction).

Poor soul, and so it is all over. But despair not. You shall yet be saved. I am too wild and nervous to write more. Do let me hear from you soon, and tell me just how you are treated now. Keep in good spirits, for all will yet be well. Miserable as I feel and bad as the weather is I have ordered the carriage and am going to talk with some lady sympathizers as to what can be done. Be brave and patient and you shall be saved.

NOTE FROM THE SAME TO GENERAL CROCKER
Gen. Crocker:

Dear Sir: Will you have the kindness to deliver the accompanying letter to Mr. Guiteau?

It is scarcely necessary for any one, especially for one of my sex, to disclaim any sympathy with Guiteau's act. If I believed he was sane at the time of the shooting of the President I could bear to see him burnt.

But I do not believe that Mr. Guiteau was of sound mind when he committed the act. It has been my fortune to see one of the most gentle and tenderest of creatures, a young girl, a clergyman's daughter, who had always so loved God as to be not only immaculate, but almost impeccable, so far carried away by a supposed divine inspiration as to contemplate and contrive a crime more heinous, under the laws of nature, than that perpetrated by Guiteau. No one, no expert, though he had been for years in daily intercourse with her, would have suspected her of having a monomania, or an insane delusion of any kind. It was reserved for me to learn from her own lips that she was a victim of a delusion that she had been commanded by God to take the life of the being, whom, next to her mother and father, she loved best on earth— her twin brother.

Many phases and features in her case and Guiteau's are analogous, and convince me that Garfield's death was not compassed by a sane, responsible mind. No adequate motive for the terrible deed has been shown. Entertaining this belief, as I do in common with thousands, I cannot help sympathizing with your prisoner. I think it would be a horrible crime to hang him.

Very respectfully yours,

CONCLUSION.

My name will be remembered as the author of this book.

Whatever this generation may think of me, future generations will see my work and record from this book. It was sown in dishonor, but the Almighty will see that it is raised in power. "Ye are honorable, but I am despised"—by fools and devils. But the Almighty will reckon with these fellows. It is a small thing that I should be judged of man's judgment. For men curse you today and bless you tomorrow.

It matters little to me whether I live three months or twenty years. Life is a flimsy dream, and it matters little when one goes. Paradise is a great improvement on this sin-cursed world, and I shall be far better off there than here.

If my case had been well tried I should not be in danger of being murdered on the gallows for executing the divine will. But what can you expect of a real estate lawyer?—a man without means or experience in the conduct of criminal causes. For these reasons, if for no other, I ought to have another chance. But it does not make much difference. My life has been a sad one and the sooner I get out of this world the better it will be for me. There is nothing in this world I want.

This book will fix my historical position, and I am content to go if the Lord wants me. But my blood will be on this nation and the officials that murder me on the gallows. If I were in the White House and General Arthur were in my place, I would pardon him though every man, woman, and child in America cursed me for it. I would do it on the ground that I believed him *insane* at the time he fired the shot, and I would let the future decide whether I was right or wrong.

FROM A BOSTON LADY.

To **Charles Guiteau.**

Today before your God you stand.
He claims you as a valiant son;
Enough; 'tis done at His command,
Repress your fears, the victory's won.

O, who should strive to learn His ways,
Profound through all the ages passed;
Enough that we obey and praise,
In these we win the crown at last.

Servant of Him who rules the sky,
The crown on earth shall yet be thine.
Hold up thy head; thy dimless eye
Yet shall behold a crown divine.

Down the dark vale thy foeman flies,
Over the lords, the wise and grand,
Over the host thou shalt arise.
Millions shall how at thy command.

www.ingramcontent.com/pod-product-compliance
Lightning Source LLC
Chambersburg PA
CBHW060238050426
42448CB00009B/1493